RETIREMENT PLANNING GUIDE

ALLIED DUNBAR
RETIREMENT PLANNING GUIDE

by

Barry Bean
Tony Foreman
and
Dr H Beric Wright

Longman

© Allied Dunbar Financial Services Ltd 1987

ISBN 0-85121-211-5

Published by

Longman Professional and Business Communications Division
Longman Group UK Limited
21–27 Lamb's Conduit Street, London WC1N 3NJ

Associated Offices

Australia	Longman Professional Publishing (Pty) Limited 130 Phillip Street, Sydney, NSW 2000
Hong Kong	Longman Group (Far East) Limited Cornwall House, 18th Floor, Taikoo Trading Estate, Tong Chong Street, Quarry Bay
Malaysia	Longman Malaysia Sdn Bhd No 3 Jalan Kilang A, Off Jalan Penchala, Petaling Jaya, Selangor, Malaysia
Singapore	Longman Singapore Publishers (Pte) Ltd 25 First Lok Yang Road, Singapore 2262
USA	Longman Group (USA) Inc 500 North Dearborn Street, Chicago, Illinois 60610

No responsibility for loss occasioned to any person acting or refraining from action as a result of the material in this publication can be accepted by the authors or publishers.

The views and opinions of Allied Dunbar may not necessarily coincide with some of the views and opinions expressed in this book which are solely those of the authors and no endorsement of them by Allied Dunbar should be inferred.

British Library Cataloguing in Publication Data
Bean, Barry
Allied Dunbar retirement planning guide.
—2nd ed.
1. Retirement—Great Britain
I. Title   II. Foreman, Tony   III. Wright, H. Beric
646.7'9   HQ164.G7

ISBN 0–85121–211–5

Printed in Great Britain by Biddles Ltd, Guildford, Surrey.

General introduction

A dictionary definition of retirement is not particularly encouraging. It talks of people who have retired as having 'withdrawn from society or observation'. It means to go away or to retreat. It confirms that to retire often means 'to leave office or employment' and then adds, somewhat darkly, 'especially because of age'.

A better approach is to regard this time of life as a time of independence. We can all be independent of the need to turn up for work regardless of whether we want to or not — but we have to accept that we have no automatic income and no automatic salary increases. We can't change our independence and choose one with better prospects and perks — the independence we achieve will only be as good as the plans we have made for it.

Many people still tend to regard this part of their life as one of 'cutting back'. They tend not to see any prospect of improvement in the quality of their life. For many executives and even for people running their own businesses, retirement, or the thought of giving up work at all, comes as a shock.

The shock is largely due to the lack of preparation. Despite the considerable and growing publicity that has been given in recent years to the need to prepare for retirement, most people still don't. They still tend to regard retirement as a time of loss and although they may not fully appreciate it, what they actually need is some careful and considered help.

Organised support for people approaching retirement has developed only gradually in this country over the last thirty years. Now, however, with an increasing tendency towards taking early retirement, there is considerably more interest being shown in the need to help people prepare themselves for what could be a twenty or twenty-five year part of their lives.

There is a climate of greater understanding emerging and more importance is being placed on careful preparation for retirement. It is estimated that approximately 10,000 people each week join the ranks of the nearly 10 million who have already retired. Retired people currently account for approximately seventeen per cent of the total population — this figure could be nearly twenty-five per cent of the population by the end of the century.

More and more companies are now adopting a more enlightened approach and helping their employees prepare for retirement — often through small group seminars arranged on behalf of the employees and their partners. A good proportion of time at these seminars is spent on the financial preparation for retirement particularly on the sort of pension they can expect from the company pension plan. Most employees are totally ignorant of what level of pension they can expect at retirement and it is something of an indictment of our approach towards our future pensioners that it has taken legislation to require employers to give their employees information about their future pensions as a right.

For most people, the basic ingredients of a happy and successful retirement are a stable environment of home, friends and interests, satisfactory health, adequate financial circumstances and a sound personal philosophy of life. Most are agreed, however, that for the majority of people approaching retirement, finance is the main concern.

The major challenge is to go on thinking positively and constructively about life. This can often be a particular problem for executives. Work offers more than just a means of earning money — it offers status and a sense of identity and for them, the loss of employment can be very similar to bereavement. The trauma may be even worse if retirement comes earlier than expected.

Beric Wright, who has contributed the section on health and philosophy to this book, is no stranger to the executive world.

He is able to draw on a wealth of experience in helping to prepare people for the 'evil day' (because that is how they look upon it), helping them to shake themselves free from the dependency on full-time employment. Having something to do, planning their time, keeping active and healthy, recognising their new found independence for what it is, are all part and parcel of helping to look at retirement as positively as possible. One of Dr Wright's constantly recurring themes is the need for couples to plan this new-found independence together. He is all too familiar with the picture of the busy executive completely immersed in his job, with bulging briefcase a regular feature of the evening and weekend conversation — or lack of it. He is aware of the re-adjustment that is necessary when husband and wife are living closely together for perhaps the first time in their lives — facing a future of 'Sunday lunch seven days a week' can often put a considerable strain on the best of relationships.

His recommendations are strongly based on reality. The statistics are relatively straightforward — men tend to marry women younger than themselves and women tend to live longer than men. The majority of planning (and certainly the majority of *financial* planning) should take into account the very high probability (but not certainty) of the wife being left on her own resources for the last years of her life. However, it is so often not done this way.

Retirement planning and life expectancy

As far as financial planning is concerned, these facts cannot be ignored if the plans are to have any chance of fulfilling their basic objective — which is to maintain a reasonable standard of living for as long as you live. Clearly, it is impossible to estimate accurately the duration of retirement, but it is also rare to make use of the information that helps to assess the probability.

The common approach is to make a simple statement about what is termed 'life expectancy'. You would tell a man of 60, for example, that his life expectancy is about 18 years. This is an interesting statistic in itself but positively unhelpful as far as financial planning is concerned. The person concerned immediately believes that his principal plans should use 18 years as a timescale.

But life expectancy does not mean that the most likely *maximum*. It means the most likely *average*. If you tell a man at 60 that he has a 50/50 chance of living *more* than 18 years, he may start to think about his financial plans in a slightly different light.

Of far more use, therefore, to the people planning for retirement are the life tables which are used by life assurance companies to calculate their premium rates. These show, not just the life expectancy of a man at any age, but the chances of him living a further 10 years, or 15 years, or 20 years, or whatever. A typical life table starts off with 100,000 individuals at birth and records how many of them die each year until, at age 100, there are virtually none left. It's a simple matter to adjust these tables so as to start off at age fifty-five or sixty and this has been done below.

Males				Expect-ancy (Years)	Females				Expect-ancy (Years)
Age					Age				
					55	1000			27.6
60	1000			18.6	60	977	1000		23.2
65	919	1000		15.1	65	939	961	1000	19.1
70	805	875	1000	11.9	70	878	899	935	15.3
75	654	712	813	9.2	75	784	802	835	11.8
80	475	516	590	6.9	80	648	663	690	8.9
85	290	315	360	5.0	85	472	483	502	6.4
90	136	148	169	3.6	90	279	285	297	4.4
95	44	48	54	2.5	95	118	121	126	3.0

The tables show how many out of 1,000 people of a particular age will live to a particular age. Because the table starts with 1,000 people in each case, it is able to show the chances of survival to any particular age. Thus, 805 out of every 1,000 men aged sixty will live to age seventy, whereas 654 will live to seventy-five and 475 to eighty. This clearly is much more useful than the simple information that the average sixty year old will live for eighteen years.

A useful feature of these tables is to follow Beric Wright's thinking and to look at the chances of survival for a husband and wife together, expessed in pure mortality terms, of course. This knowledge is absolutely vital for sensible planning.

Let's take the case of a husband aged sixty and a wife aged fifty-five — which represents a typical retirement age of a husband and a typical age difference between husband and wife. The table shows that:

- 654 out of every 1,000 men aged sixty will live to age seventy-five.
- 878 out of every 1,000 women of age fifty-five will live to age seventy.

It follows that (if we assume that they are all married) 87.8 per cent of the wives of the 654 surviving men will also be alive.

That means that 574 couples will survive or, put another way, there will be eighty widowers and 304 widows.

In nearly two thirds of the cases, either the husband or wife will have died after twenty years of retirement. The survivor may have another ten years to look forward to and this is often overlooked in financial planning. Most men almost take it for granted that 'the survivor' will be their wife. However, for those couples where only one life survives twenty years, one fifth of those survivors will be the male life.

Tony Foreman and **Barry Bean**, in their chapters on investment planning, examine a wide range of issues from the choice of investment to the increasingly popular idea of retiring abroad. They lay a lot of stress on the need to keep plans flexible and to make sure that a careful distinction is drawn between immediate financial needs and longer term planning for income.

The key word of course is 'planning'. The road to hell may be paved with good intentions but it was never more true when planning for our own independence. There are so many things which need to be planned for: continuing an income, preserving the family home, avoiding unnecessary taxation and avoiding unnecessary family disputes and turmoil. Despite the real rewards of planning for the future most problems arise, not because people have made incorrect plans but because they have made no plans at all. Even the most successful of businessmen can damage his own independence by inactivity and neglect.

An American put it better — 'we don't plan to fail, we simply fail to plan'.

In the other books in the *Allied Dunbar* series (particularly the best selling *Tax Guide*) there is frequently a chapter or list of ideas on how to save tax, or how best to arrange your affairs. In the same spirit, but with a slight variation, here's a list of popular fallacies about planning for your future independence.

Planning for the future, according to popular belief:

- is only for couples
- is only for the rich
- is only for the elderly
- is expensive
- is not for wives or members of the family
- is simply a matter of making a will
- is a once-in-lifetime job
- is only concerned with life assurance

We are all living longer. Medical care is better, we look after ourselves more with diet and exercise, modern surgery can help to refurbish some of the worn out bits — and we are retiring earlier.

It's time to start planning for it.

Contents

Page

General Introduction   v

PART ONE: HEALTH

1   Problems and priorities in retirement   **3**

Facing retirement   3
The demographic scene   6
Attitudes and activities   10
    How to spend your time   12
    Gainful or voluntary activity   13
More about moving house   17
Relationships, roles and anxieties   19
    Useful addresses   23

2   Mental outlook and relationships   **25**

The framework   25
Stress and relaxation   28
    Sleep   30
Relationships   32
Sex after sixty   35

3   Keeping physically fit   **37**

   Arthritis, rheumatism and mobility   39
   Keeping in good trim   41
   Warning signs and symptoms   41
   Diet and digestion   43
        Salt   45

4   Seeing and hearing   **47**

   Sight   47
   Hearing   48
   Better hearing for the elderly   49
   by Dafydd Stephens and Lorraine Jeffrey Nicol
        Introduction   49
        What to do if you have hearing problems   50
        Hearing aids   51
        Other aids to hearing   52
        Conclusions   53
   Tinnitus   54
   by Dafydd Stephens and Lorraine Jeffrey Nicol
        Introduction   54
        What should you do if you have tinnitus?   55
        Conclusions   57
   Teeth   57
   by K J Lewis, FDS

5   Special problem areas   **63**

   Special problems — women   63
   Special problems — men   66

6   Accommodation in retirement   **69**

   by Bill Loving
   A general note   69
   Moving or staying   70
   Finding a new home   72
   Life on the level — a flat or bungalow   74
   Mobile homes   75
   Sheltered and not-so-sheltered housing   76
   Sources of further information   78

PART TWO: FINANCIAL ASPECTS

7	**Introduction**	**83**
	Drawing up a budget	85
	Asking yourself the right questions	86

8	**Funding your retirement**	**89**
	Why is advance planning so vital?	89
	Assumptions	90
	Why are pension schemes the most time efficient form of saving?	91
	What types of pension are available?	92
	Company pension schemes	92
	Personal pension schemes	94
	Self-employed pensions	96
	What can you do to improve the pension that you will receive from a former employer?	96
	Transfer values	97
	Buy-out bonds	97
	Future legislation	97
	Can you fund a pension for your wife?	98
	What is the best way to save out of surplus income?	99
	Tax efficient capital investments	101
	What can be done at the last minute?	103

9	**Planning your pension**	**105**
	State pensions	105
	Basic retirement pension	106
	Graduated pension	106
	State earnings related scheme	106
	Self-employed persons	108
	Private pensions	108
	Choosing a pension	108
	Commuting your company pension for cash	109
	Is commuting pensions worthwhile?	110
	Pensions and inflation	110
	Personal pension plans	111

Open market options 112
Widow's pension 112
Invalidity benefit 112

10 Tax does matter **115**

Working out your tax bill 115
Income tax 115
How is age allowance computed? 118
Capital gains tax 119
Tax planning 123
Choosing the right retirement date 124
Timing of retirement 125
CGT on the sale of your business/private
company 126
How can you minimise tax in the year of
retirement? 127
Checklist for year of retirement 128

11 Carry on working **129**

How much can you earn without affecting your state
pension? 129
What happens if you defer taking your state pension? 130
What happens if you do not draw your company
pension right away? 130
How will your part-time earnings be assessed for tax
purposes? 131
Starting a new business 131
National Insurance contributions 132
How can you save tax? 132

12 Managing your money **135**

What are the main criteria to use when evaluating an
investment 135
Personal circumstances 137
Analysis 139
Tax 140
Inflation 141

13 Interest bearing investments **145**

Building societies   145
Government stock   146
Index-linked government stock   149
Offshore roll-up funds   150
National Savings   151
    National Savings Income Bonds   151
    National Savings Indexed Income Bond   151
    National Savings Deposit Bond   151
    National Savings Certificates   151
Index-Linked National Savings Certificates   152
Insurance company schemes   153
    Annuities   154
    Annuity home income schemes   155

14 Equity and property investments **157**

Equities   158
    Your own portfolio   160
    Unit trusts   160
Investment bonds   163
    Tax on cashing in the bond   164
    Partial cashing in   164
    Types of fund   165
    Flexibility   167

15 Investment Strategy **169**

Some general principles   171
    Investments should be managed   172
    Invest in unit trusts for income   172
    Consistency counts   173
    Tax and your investments   174
    Putting these principles into practice   175

16 Retiring on a low income **179**

Supplementary pension   179
Other help   180
    Going into hospital   180
    Local authorities and other organisations   180

A capital idea   181
Addresses   181
Some leaflets you may find helpful   182

17 Making a Will   183

Intestacy   183
The formalities   184
    Choosing executors   185
    The importance of flexibility   186
    The alternative   187
Summary   188

18 Passing on your wealth   189

How is IHT charged on death?   189
    Main exemptions   191
    Transfers to your spouse   191
    Gifts to charities   191
    Gifts for national purposes   191
    Special reliefs   191
    How are lifetime gifts treated?   192
    Gifts into trust   196
    Deeds of covenant   198
    Taking advantage of the seven year rule   199
    Drawing up your Will to minimise IHT   201
    Equalising your estates   202

19 Off to the sun — retirement abroad   203

What do you have to do to satisfy the Inland Revenue
    that you are not resident?   203
Residence   204
    Available accommodation   204
    Visits to the UK   205
    Husband and wife treated separately   206
Ordinary residence   206
    Claims under double tax treaties   206
How does the concept of domicile differ from
    residence and why is it so important?   208

What tax planning steps can be taken in the year of
   departure? 210
      Golden handshakes 211
      Commutation of pension rights 211
      Capital gains tax 211
How will your UK income be taxed when you are
   residence overseas? 212
      Directors' fees and pensions 213
      Dividends 214
      Interest 215
      Exempt gilts 215
      Rental income 216
      Offshore investment companies 217
      Personal allowances 217
What do you need to find out about the country in
   which you are going to live? 218
      General strategy — finding out more 218
      Other financial considerations 218
      Foreign exchange controls 219
      Inheritance law 219
      Purchase of a property overseas 220

20 Homeward bound **223**

UK expatriates returning home 223
   Checklist for expatriates about to return to the
      UK 223
      Golden handshakes 224
Retiring to the UK — a tax haven! 225
      Inheritance tax planning 227

Glossary 229

Appendix 235

Leaflets available from any HM Inspector of Taxes office

Index 237

Part One
Health

1 Problems and priorities in retirement

Facing retirement

Not long ago at a small pre-retirement seminar for senior managers and their spouses, we had — with the aid of the ubiquitous flip chart — an enlightening discussion. Each of the participants was asked to suggest a problem or priority in their retirement thinking so far. One of the wives surprisingly came up with the vital need to have a plan for each day. 'To make it worth getting up for', her husband remarked.

This is in practice one of the critical decisions about retirement. Some fear it, others resent it and an increasing number look forward to the last day at work. I can speak personally from both the academic and the practical angles because after twenty years of struggle to make the Pre-Retirement Association (PRA) viable, I personally retired from full-time, largely managerial work, four years ago. I was fairly certain that I knew what to plan and had collected more than enough commitments to keep me involved. But having had a round of embarrassingly friendly social retirement events, I suddenly found that on the day after my sixty-fifth birthday, I had nothing to do. The diary was blank: there was no office to go to, nothing specific to be responsible for and no secretary to organise my day.

In spite of all my knowledge and homework, it was a shock and although I still had contacts and non-executive roles, I did feel lost for several months. It took this time to learn to restructure my life, adjust to new priorities of my own making and, I hope, become a more relaxed person. And of course I was lucky because I did have several different roles, some new things to take up and additional income from some of them. Interestingly, too, about three months later I suddenly realised that I felt quite different — and very much better. I realised that I was no longer chronically tired. Busy people as they get older learn to function effectively against a background of considerable fatigue, not properly relieved by the holiday quota.

I can assure readers that being busy and involved, but not over-tired, is a major benefit of retirement. You suddenly real-ise, as I did, that over the last few years you were seldom at your best.

I do not want to boast or preach too hard and will, after this, stop reminiscing, but it struck me that a less well-prepared per-son who really was faced with blank weeks stretching ahead would probably feel bemused, sad and lost.

Part of my advice on contingency planning for retirement, and in my view quite the most important part, is to realise that work not only pays the rent and provides a standard of living but, more importantly, is responsible for one's status and identity. Without this a retired person is in danger of becoming a 'non-person'. As such he and his wife are in danger of drifting rud-derless in a sea of trivial and meaningless pursuits. They may well lose their disciplines, and become indulgent lotus eaters surrounded by other 'non-people'.

A second critical benefit of work is that it provides association with other people. You may not like them much but at least they are there, even if only to rail against. It is a fact of life that people need people and appreciate being wanted. Loneliness we know is the main emotional problem of getting older, par-ticularly if you live alone, or you are unmarried.

All of which is why the seminar wife talked such sense when she said 'we must have things planned to do'. There must be entries in the diary. As she and her husband had not yet retired, this showed a great deal of insight and understanding. They should have no major problems.

Over the years of talking, writing and advising about retire-ment, we have established that the main areas of decision are as follows, and they make quite a tidy branched logic or critical path picture. They are in strict order:

(1) What are you going to do, how do you propose to spend your days?
(2) Where will you be able, or want, to do these things?
(3) What sort of house will be best as your base, ie, should you move to a smaller house or even a bungalow?
(4) How much money will you have or need to live on and would it be sensible to earn more?
(5) What about your health and what should you know and do to optimise it? There is, in fact, a lot you can and should do.

To this very basic checklist, I think it is worth adding a further point which is the need to review relationships with one's spouse, the rest of the family and the social circle. Most wives look forward to seeing more of their husbands and having time together. But if communication has been poor and the relationship a bit negative, there may be a strain. Marriage may be for better or worse but not for most of us at the level of seven lunches a week. This implies a lot of role change and rethinking.

Clearly too, family needs and priorities will influence decisions under the first three headings and must be thought through. After the war when we started a family my mother, who was a busy doctor, announced firmly that she had brought up four children and was not going to do it again. She was an academic but rather inactive grandparent. Most of you will probably be looking forward to more involvement but there are pitfalls and you must beware of losing too much of your independence. However, family needs may play a large part in determining, for instance, where you want to live.

Finance and money management are the kernel of this book and require the best possible advice. I can say this with some experience because one knows that professional people, particularly doctors, tend to be bad at looking after their own affairs. And businessmen may be better at making — and possibly spending — money, than they are at managing it for their old age.

But I should like to end this section on a note of caution, perhaps prejudiced by my own attitudes and somewhat puritanical approach. Over the years I have been worried by the impression that a lot of people look forward to retirement as a continuous holiday. Enough money, no responsibilities, swimming and drinking in the sun and so on: all made easier by the financial benefits of the Costa Somewhere.

This may be fine for some but by retiring to Spain you are opting for a very negative life: pure pleasure, without involvement or responsibility becomes very boring and remote from the real world. A recent article by a friend of mine, who really ought to have known better, listed all the sybaritic virtues of Spain — golf, swimming, cards, drinks, sun, etc. But do you really want to be a useless person retreating into an unreal enclave of non-contributory life? If you do opt for a foreign residence it is both prudent and civil to take the trouble to learn about the country and to speak the language. To live permanently somewhere and not be able to communicate with the citizens is both arrogant and insulting.

My personal advice is remain in local circulation, go on contributing to society and only holiday on the Costas.

The demographic scene

Although the frail and lonely elderly have long been recognised as a group in the population requiring support and shelter, it is only over the last twenty-five years that the retired group has become recognised as presenting separate and different problems and needs. In about 1960 the National Corporation for the Care of Old People began to feel that the 'young elderly' needed specific thought and advice. They set up a broadly based exploratory group called the Pre-Retirement Advisory Committee.

This group, of which I was a member, established, at least to its own satisfaction, that this was a problem area requiring attention. Consequently we set up on our own as the Pre-Retirement Association and had a long hard struggle to establish an independent base and develop the requisite support.

What has happened in demographic terms is that many more people are living longer. Initially it was not so much that life expectancy was increasing, as that more and more people were living out their full term. This in itself was nearer four than three score years and ten. Since then life expectancy is beginning to increase so that we now have a situation in which large numbers of people remain active until well after eighty and those in sheltered housing are often in their nineties.

Taking the population as a whole and adding in the move towards earlier retirement and, sadly, redundancy, we have a situation in which roughly a third of the population are retired and living on pensions. The parallel growth of occupational pensions has also to a degree increased the incomes of this group.

When, for instance, we started the retirement magazine *Choice*, we were told that it was doomed because there would be no advertising revenue as the target readers had no disposable income and were all on the breadline. This proved, as we suspected it would, to be nonsense and after a spluttering start the magazine has proved to be a useful success and now has competitors but no serious rivals.

It has succeeded because it provides specific advice (for those about to retire, or who have recently retired) on finance, housing, health and activities. What has been constantly encouraging is the accounts by retired people of all the fascinating and exciting things they have managed to do: some of them for purely constructive and contributory pleasure, others as second, or even third careers, to supplement their incomes.

What has happened is that better housing, higher standards of nutrition and health care have reduced the toll of deaths in childhood and middle age. Thus more people retire in fair health and, given sensible management of their lives, can now expect to live twenty or more years in retirement. But much more important is the realisation that these 'young elderly' people may well have ten to fifteen years of vigorous potential. They are in no way frail or feeble and are capable of considerable activity and contribution.

It is critical that you, as an about-to-be or recently retired individual, realise this. You are *not* going on the shelf to waste away: you may well deteriorate if you don't try. Given, however, the will and the determination, you can go on much as before. Brain and muscle power can be preserved and developed, but this must be done as a conscious policy and you must not allow yourself to drift without targets.

This same population trend is true of all the developed countries which are increasingly working towards the provision of better recognition of, and facilities for, the retired. In America, for instance, they have raised the retirement age but I doubt if this is the right way round the course. The pace of administrative, business and productive life is now such that most kitchens get too hot for the sixty year olds. In any case, the route to the top must be kept open for younger people.

What is still required in this country are better facilities for part-time work, the total abolition of the earnings rule and a better advisory network about involvement at a variety of levels. It would clearly be politically dangerous and socially undesirable for a third of the population to become separated, isolated and aggrieved. Equally it is sensible that they should remain more or less evenly distributed across the country and not collected into retirement enclaves.

Obviously some parts of the country and indeed other countries, like Spain, have a better climate and a more pleasant environment but it is unwise in my view to encourage the development of large concentrations of retired people, as in Florida and, to a degree, our own south coast. If integration and involvement in the local community are the keys, groups of inward-looking older people must be dangerous for themselves and the local community.

I have watched the drift to Spain and similar places with alarm. It may be fine to spend a year or five lazing in the sun and getting better value for your money but before taking this decision it is wise to think ahead to ten or fifteen years hence. What will it be like to be a foreigner growing old in another country, surrounded by a diminishing group of ageing expatriates dreaming of home and the good old days and increasingly losing touch with home and family? In this connection the problems of illness and frailty have also to be faced. Adequate medical care and resources must be available wherever you are. These problems are discussed in Chapter 5.

There is another demographic problem that bears on this,

which is the fact that, for reasons we don't understand, women live appreciably longer than men. This means that part of your contingency planning for late retirement must include thought not only about possible frailty but also about what will happen when there is only one of you. Life in Spain, for instance, for an elderly widow must be a fearful thought, compared with being near the family or in a granny flat or Abbeyfield house, close to friends.

Because of this longevity and greater potential for activity, it has recently become apparent that we need to rephrase our advice about retirement planning. It is now clear that it is probably sensible to think about and plan for two distinct phases of retirement.

The first is obviously the phase of activity and involvement with very little diminution of faculties but more opportunities for doing the things that you both want to do, at a reduced pace and not under time pressure. In this respect I can assure you that once over the readjustment, busy though you may be, it is liberating to know that you don't have to do anything you don't like or feel behoven about. Everything you take on is your own choice and can be dropped tomorrow if it does not suit or becomes frustrating. For this phase, it may not be necessary to make much adjustment in lifestyle or living. You will probably find that your money goes further than you thought it would. The mortgage may be paid off, school fees finished, National Insurance and pension contributions stopped and so on. Income may drop but so does tax, so that on balance you are less worse off than you feared. I know that there are financial advantages in having a mortgage but psychologically there is a lot to be said for being and feeling free and this may help your spouse. If you want to earn a bit and were previously salaried, there are tax advantages in being self-employed.

Having decided, as previously outlined, what you are going to do and where, the next vital point is housing. If you decide to stay put, your present house may well do for the time being or longer. But if it is too big, has or has not a garden and so on, there may be a case for a smaller or more appropriate house in more or less the same area.

If you decide to move, for family or other reasons, the pros and cons of which are discussed later, it is worth giving a lot of thought to the sort of house that will carry you into phase two, ie, given a choice there is a case for thinking ahead and remembering that there may come a time when stairs are difficult, you may not be able to drive and ultimately there will only be one of you. In essence, however, little change may be needed and I am strongly in favour of staying where your social roots are.

Phase two, the period of frailty and diminished mobility, may require change. As I have said, if change is decided earlier on, the phases may be merged but if not, more special accommodation will have to be provided and a possible move nearer better medical facilities or to a sheltered housing unit. I do know of one family who are now in their third generation of granny flat occupation, with the younger generation taking over the main house and their parents in comfortable independence round the side. All this may sound gloomy but I can assure you that it is best thought about in good time.

The real message in these first two sections is that as you are likely to be about for another twenty years, it is far too long a time to drift about doing nothing in particular. Retirement does provide opportunities and challenges to restructure your lives and it is the meeting of new challenges that keeps you young and lively. Grasping this nettle requires thought and effort but it is well worth it. An increasing number of eighty year olds remain in active circulation and I do hope that you will opt for this alternative.

Doing little and living in the emotional past is not the best recipe for survival.

Attitudes and activities

The other day I met a friend who had been retired about a year and he looked very well, cheerful and lively. After telling me about all the things that he and his wife were doing, he finished up by saying that looking back a little he was wondering how he ever had time to work. This seemed to me to be an ideal state in retirement. As you will read in the more detailed health section, health is very much a function of well-being and if morale and satisfaction are high, there is no time to be ill or dis-eased.

There are all sorts of facets to early retirement but the most important thing is to accept it, at the lowest level of resentment as a necessity. At the highest level, it should, if not positively welcomed, be regarded as an opportunity to re-plan life and priorities and do new things.

The person who drifts into retirement with a feeling of resentment, will be miserable, no fun to be with and is very likely to become depressed and dis-eased. These are the people who don't draw their pensions for long — they fade away.

In the Pre-Retirement Association we preach that retirement planning should start about five years before the day. This may be a bit idealistic but the experts do say that the best financial planning does have this lead time. But as an alleged expert in the behavioural aspects of retirement I would advocate serious thought and discussion being given to the problems, and plans laid to deal with them, at least two years ahead. A few companies facilitate this by building in a diminishing working week over the last year or six months. In this way the job has been taken over and you are used to filling the non-working days: and your spouse will be getting used to having you around.

There are several good reasons for this advice. The first and probably most important is that it gently conditions you to the thought, starts you on the planning trail, begins to generate things to look forward to and minimises the chances of becoming bored and resentful.

Second is that if you decide to move to a new area, which may be a risky business and is discussed later, you can get this organised and begin to grow new social roots and get to know people and possibilities. If you already have a second home which you propose to make your new base, this is a much lesser problem. The nicest thing that happened to us when we gave up London, was an invitation to a drink next door which turned out to be a friendly event to welcome us full time to the village. As we had considered selling the house because it was rather large, it was particularly encouraging to be welcomed — we had made the right decision.

The third reason is the possibility of beginning to learn new skills and develop a wider range of interests and activities. As I have said, activities and involvements are critical and they don't just happen; they have to be planned. We do have in this country, although it is creaking a bit under government austerity, a fine adult education network which is there to be used.

I aim this advice particularly at the workaholic and the professional person with few outside interests apart from those which are work-related. Not only are you likely to be a rather boring person, you will find it more difficult to maintain morale and establish a new identity. It is also worth noting that old dogs can learn new tricks — and skills — but only if they are prepared to try.

To reiterate the crux of my message, you must be prepared for retirement and have a discipline of physical and mental stimulation. So, against this background, what are you going to do and what will be in your diary? The possibilities are legion and you have to decide your priorities.

How to spend your time

For both of you, assuming that you are married, these choices are critical and should, I suggest, be made fairly flexible because as the situation evolves your views may change with experience. It seems sensible initially to take on slightly too much over the first year. This helps the transition from work to retirement and can provide a range of choice after about a year, ie, you can weed out one or two commitments that turn out to be boring, too demanding or involve a lot of travel. It is also important to realise that if what you want to do is professional or work-related, it is wise to get it organised at an early stage. Several people I know have been surprised by how quickly they were forgotten. It seems easier to remain in circulation than to get back into it again. Some years ago I met a man who had gone off on a nine month world tour and returned to find many of his possible slots filled.

It is wise at this stage to make a rough decision as to how much time you want to spend together, do things jointly, and the extent to which your activities should be separate. It is probably unwise, for instance, for both of you to be on the same committee!

At a recent seminar, the point was made that it was easy to step into the position of being an exploited grandparent: the children taking the view that now you are retired you can be considered a convenient dumping ground. Your schedules can easily be disorganised by too much baby-sitting and you may find that large doses of young grandchildren are exhausting. It may be helpful in this respect not to have too many spare bedrooms.

Obviously this decision rests largely with the wife but she should remember my mother's view and on the whole lead her own life. Clearly if there is a family health crisis or marriage break-up priorities may have to be altered.

Professional people, such as doctors, accountants, lawyers and senior managers, do have the advantage that because of their qualifications and experience they can go on working either at a reduced rate or in a consultancy or non-executive role. It is, however, surprisingly difficult to switch from the executive to non-executive role in your old firm and I suspect that for both parties it should not continue for more than a very few years.

It is also important that the temptation to continue exactly as before should be resisted. It is much more stimulating to do new things, work on a different network and perhaps acquire new skills and interests.

Another factor in settling these priorities is to have a clear idea as to how far and how often you are prepared to travel and be away from home. In my view this should be minimised because travel, and driving in particular, becomes more demanding as you get older.

Gainful or voluntary activity

You will already have done a rough budget for your retirement and should thus know whether or not it is essential for you to supplement your pension and savings on a regular basis. This decision clearly determines your priorities, what you look for and possibly where you live.

I would suggest that the younger you are the more you are likely to need income and indeed the more sensible it is to have the disciplines of an earnings-related commitment; part-time work can be rewarding. If the need for income is marginal, you can opt for a range of voluntary or caring activities which may well pay expenses, and be pleased when the odd fee or gainful chore comes along.

Wives and single people will have to make similar decisions and it may well be easier for women to find part-time paid work. But the decisions having been taken, the next step is to look around for contacts to get you suitably involved and enrol in training or educational courses.

Gainful activity

It is obviously not sensible to try to list all the various ways in which it might be possible to find a part- or full-time job which uses your experience and meets your inclinations, but several points are worth making.

First, probably the easiest way, at least in theory, is to start a new enterprise or offer a service. This requires imagination, guts and a bit of capital, but with your experience you ought to know how to run a business and control stock and cashflow. The pages of *Choice* magazine over the years are full of successful second careers, usually at the service level.

Secondly, there are a number of organisations which exist to help older people find jobs at various levels and some of these are listed at the end of this chapter.

Thirdly, it is wise to accept that any job you take on is likely to be at a lower level than you were used to and, indeed, you probably want less responsibility, particularly for staff. It has often worried me that business and managerial people sadly made redundant tend to look for, and usually fail to find, jobs at their previous level. One needs to be prepared to start again and justify one's skills rather than be taken at a possibly tarnished face value. In all sections of our community there is still a huge need for services and to get things done reliably at a reasonable rate. If I needed to do this, for example, I would start a jobbing gardening facility and trundle my spade and mower round, tidying up and fixing the garden for the frail and disinclined. There is a crying need for this, certainly on the fringes of the larger cities and even in the country.

Fourthly, there is the vital need for association with other people to replace one's 'old work mates' and this is where service activities are both important and useful. Even working part-time in a shop provides lots of contacts, if also a few frustrations.

Our world is full of things which need to be done and there are plenty of people about able and willing to pay for these. It may sound menial but could be exciting and rewarding. One of my dreams, and we nearly did it once some years ago, is to start a community based activities centre or facility exchange. People who wanted to do things would bring in their skills and others wanting a service would buy it or contribute something different. One or two units like this do exist and flourish. Why not consider starting one on your patch?

I make no apology for the fact that what I have outlined here is both obvious and to a degree platitudinous but what I have tried to do is very simply to set out some alternatives to start you thinking.

Voluntary work

Here again the scope is endless. Our society is largely based on self-help as distinct from Local Authority welfare. There is a host of organisations providing this assistance from, say, the National Trust to Meals on Wheels and Day Centres. They need both workers and administrators and organisers. Many also need fund raisers but this is a difficult task which does not often appeal.

It may sound a bit pious but I do think that it is reasonable to urge competent and previously busy people to seriously consider ploughing something back into the community. This can be both necessary and very rewarding because we all need to be wanted and to have others relying on us. Your contacts and contributions may even help your own old age.

There are lots of local and national bodies crying out for participation and my own favourite example is the Abbeyfield Society. This consists of a countrywide network of autonomous local societies working on a common formula, providing homes for the lonely elderly. Each society is financially and administratively independent. It acquires houses which are converted into six or more bedsits with a housekeeper, and provides a home for those requiring care and company. As the need is growing, Abbeyfield requires all the organisational help and support it can get, particularly from the recently retired. This is to start new societies and to take over from older members to give committees new blood. One must remember that this type of voluntary work is just as valuable to the participants as it is to those who benefit directly from the charitable service provided.

There cannot be any community or part of the country where there is not some need for more help and in most areas there are organisations, like the local Council of Voluntary Services, Citizens Advice Bureaux, Town Hall, public library and so on which will tell you about what is available.

As with my suggestions about activities centres, there is a need for setting up groups of retired people to support each other, discuss problems and do things — both active and social. Such a group, once established, could put pressure on the locality to provide more facilities for the retired, from part-time jobs or educational courses, to special physical activity sessions in keep-fit and swimming.

Amusing yourself

As well as the types of involvement outlined so far, you need to plan time to do a number of your own things. All the 'things' you have always wanted to do but never had time for. They can be active or passive, indoors or out and, preferably, both mental and physical.

It is sensible to leave enough time to enjoy yourself and develop new skills and hobbies. These will become more important as you get less active and less inclined to charge about on committees and to travel around. It is also important to build in time each day for some physical activity which will help to keep you fit and supple.

The trick, I am sure, is to hold a balance between the personal or domestic activities and wider involvement, and to have enough time for both. But I do think that it is dangerous to plan only for recreation: more of it certainly, but not full-time. I don't really believe that golf is enough of a full-time activity for intelligent people. And this is really why I worry about the concept of joining a retirement enclave in a warm country. Life may be pleasant, money may go a bit further, but it is barren and non-contributory, which must become boring and inward-looking.

More about moving house

If you look up bereavement in the dictionary it gives the meaning as 'to be deprived of'. I have already made the point that, unless properly handled and understood, work bereavement can bring the same consequences as perhaps the death of a spouse, depression, loneliness, guilt and resentment, etc. If at the same time you move to a new area because it seems a nicer place to live, you run the risk of double bereavement because you are a newcomer to a strange land.

The cottage down the lane, so lovely in the summer, may be less attractive ten years later in the winter, when you can no longer drive a car and have to carry home the shopping, or when there is only one of you living alone.

A couple of years ago we had a detailed and poignant case study from a couple who moved north two years after retirement to be near their daughter. Although they had thought through the problems and knew what they were facing, it took them two traumatic and lonely years to begin to grow roots in the new area and several times they nearly came back.

Retirement is a time when you need all the social contacts you have, to establish your new identity and activities. Thus by moving, the dice are loaded against you and it is difficult, particularly for older women, to establish a new social network. For this range of reasons our overall advice from the Pre-Retirement Association is to very careful about moving and to be strongly biased in favour of staying where you have mostly been. Of course there may be good reasons, like not wanting to be too much in a town, being nearer the family, a more clement part of the country, cheaper living, and so on, for moving but as a generalisation it is usually wiser to stay put, in perhaps a smaller or more appropriate house in the same locality.

With people being so much more fit and active into their seventies no change may be needed for some years but if you do decide to change it is wise to think ahead to potential frailty.

Thus a bungalow, smaller house, flat with a good lift, etc, may be sensible. It also provides an opportunity to reconsider activities like gardening. Now is the chance to have a larger or smaller garden depending on preference.

A last point about moving is that if you want to do this there is a great deal to be said for trying to start the change a year or more before retirement by establishing a second home well in advance. An increasing number of people do so by having a weekend home out of town, with perhaps a much smaller work-related residence in town which is easy to give up. Again, particularly in terms of retirement, it is often easier to find modest part-time work in a small community. I have always been worried about too much commuting for older busy people which is an argument in favour of two homes if you can afford it.

Having said this, however, one does find that living in two places produces problems and we were always carting food, clothes, animals, etc, in and out of town. It was a great relief when this stopped and, as I have said, we did have contacts and activities in the village.

The value of your house or houses is another critical factor. For many people the lump sum of your pension and the paid-for house are your main assets and must be considered as part of the financial planning. It may well be wise, particularly later on, to consider capitalising the property to improve your financial comfort. In these days most of our children are doing at least as well as, and often better than we did at their age. They would rather have less worry about us than be left a large house to be sold. There is much advice about this topic in Part Two of this book.

At the time of writing we, in BUPA Hospitals, are selecting residents for a new pilot project in sheltered housing for the frail elderly who cannot cope on their own. One of the things we have to do is to make a financial assessment. In pursuit of this an old lady recently seen was reluctant to sell her quite large house because she wanted to leave something for her nephew. The nephew when contacted, with her permission, as he was the executor, was quite clear that he and his wife would be far happier to have their old aunt contented and comfortable, than hold out for the money. It is worth noting too that this conflict could have been mitigated several years earlier by more open discussion.

I have laboured the points about where to live because they are critical in retirement planning. They clearly relate to priorities about activities and being near the family and tend to be taken without properly thinking through their implications. It is also prudent to consider the time base involved and know whether you are planning for the rest of your lives, or a shorter period, followed later by somewhere simpler and more supportive. In this respect, it is wise to make the changes a little too soon rather than cope with, or even contemplate, the change involved at the onset of frailty or in response to a crisis.

Relationships, roles and anxieties

Retirement can impose a severe strain on the relationship between husband and wife. If you stop to think about it, married couples do not, on the whole, see all that much of each other. Weekends and holidays provide some opportunity for communication and joint activities but in relation to the rest of the year this is a small proportion of the time. If in addition the husband does a lot of travelling, brings work home and is out three or four evenings a week, the situation becomes more difficult.

I suspect that the overall situation has improved in the last decade but suddenly being thrown together can produce a strain on a neutral or not very strong relationship, particularly as the type of man involved is likely to be a workaholic with a wife who has allowed him to get away with relative non-participation for so long.

This is why I have laid so much emphasis on planning activities and establishing — or re-establishing — relationships within the family. The lack of these may be a reason why a few men, and possibly working women too, fear retirement and go on hoping that it will not happen to them. There is, therefore, subject to the need to remain in circulation, a case to be made for the equivalent of a second honeymoon.

As a culture we are not particularly good at adult relationships, with each other, with our own parents and with the children.

Mothers tend to fret about the way in which their young conduct their lives and bring up the grandchildren. Many of them make this worse by continuing to see their children as still obedient and grateful but not as adults living their own lives. The relationship, therefore, becomes more of a duty than a pleasure.

There is a genuine conflict here because the young are brought up, educated and pushed out into the world to be independent. This is fine and far better than having them exploiting their parents, not marrying, living at home and getting their shirts washed: the modern equivalent of the younger unmarried daughter who devoted her life to her mother and ended up in middle age as a lost soul without the experience of a real life of her own.

Equally, however, in social terms the family unit, and now the extended family, is critical for social stability. And a supportive family network is the best way to keep the frail elderly out of the clutches of the social workers and the Welfare State. To achieve at least some of this, the relationships have to be based on mutual respect and appreciation and not just a sense of duty.

The problems involved are, of course, long-term and dependent to a degree on the attitudes handed on to the next generation — but they do need to be worked on. In the section on health and well-being I have argued the case for more open relationships and a willingness to discuss problems, grievances and differences in a non-threatening and non-confrontational way. Our national non-emotional approach and the stiff upper lip militate against this openness. 'Carry on as before and pretend it is not there', may work when there is plenty to do but in retirement there may not be enough glue left to make the relationship stick.

I have already made the point that a decision has to be taken about how active you want to become as grandparents and there is no doubt that the generation gap makes for easy and joyful relationships between the older and the younger, provided of course that it does not produce conflicts with the parents in the middle.

What I am really urging at this point is that thought should be given to discussing differences before they become grievances and establishing some ground rules for minimising anxiety and developing a constructive social network to which all contribute. Without such a contribution you are unlikely to be wanted or appreciated and without it you are likely to be lonely, which is the biggest single problem of growing old gracefully. All this is why I am on the whole against a retirement pattern based almost entirely on recreation: be this the golf course in this country or the patio abroad. Real people in everyday situations provide a better stimulus and challenge than being a non-contributory drone.

What will happen when one of us gets ill and dies is inevitably something we all think about — or should do as we get older. This again requires discussion. It is, however, worrying to find the number of quite senior people who have not made or updated their wills: equally the number of wives, who are the most likely survivors, who may not know (1) where the will is, (2) who the solicitor is, (3) the executors and, most important, (4) how they are to pay next month's bills and what there will be to live on.

I think it is irresponsible not to discuss this situation and there is a case for the will, or some of it, to be the matter of a family council so that everyone knows where they stand. Bereavement is tragic and difficult enough, especially for the less resilient elderly. It can be made much easier to cope with if there is a plan to bring into action. If there is no such plan and nowhere set to go, it is wise to struggle on and avoid taking vital decisions until some of the emotional dust has settled and things are seen more clearly.

With grown-up children, houses are an under-used asset, empty soon after breakfast, tidied up an hour later and waiting for the evening. With the husband in and out all day the functional nature of the house changes, which changes and their implications, the wife must tolerate and even encourage. Soon after we opened our first Pre-Retirement Association offices in Clapham, a nice man walked in and asked if he could help in any way. His offer was taken up and he soon became an appreciated member of our new family. It transpired that, recently retired and on a small pension, he was turned out of the house by his wife after breakfast and told not to come back until lunchtime. All he could afford to do was to wander about or sit and gaze. Rather like the retired workman who watches his old mates go into work and then counts the bricks on the wall opposite his window.

Extreme cases these may be but at different levels they do illustrate a lack of understanding of the domestic changes in retirement. A well-organised non-working woman will have found a range of outside activities as the children grow up: indeed if she does little but housework she is likely to be bored, boring and vulnerable — but this is another story. But the last thing the wife should do is to give up her activities to look after her retired husband. What ought to happen is that, metaphorically, he should go on a cooking course, sweep the stairs and learn to iron shirts.

In this approach there is a generation gap. Our children are now sharing more of the domestic chores, doing the shopping and even some cooking from time to time; and very competently too. Retirement does give a chance, and includes a need, to re-think domestic roles and priorities and incorporate a greater degree of sharing than our generation was used to. This in itself is a new challenge and stimulus.

Not many men now expect to have their domestic lives served up without contribution but a few still do and their wives to a degree think that they justify their existence by being the waitress. I suspect, however, that the relationship will be better with more joint activity and such changes will be facilitated by some insight into what is required.

There will be more leisure and more time together. The main point I have been trying to make is that with the loss of work, relationships become more precious and do need nourishing. Like the whole of retirement planning, the changes are unlikely 'just to happen' but have to be contrived. With a third of the population retired, we have to demonstrate that we can and want to remain active and contributory members of society and that our experience and wisdom are useful and not threatening.

Useful addresses

Association of Researchers into Voluntary Action and Community Involvement (ARVAC)
Stephen Hatch (Chairman)
26 Queens Road
Wivenhoe
Essex CO7 9DL

Action Resource Centre
Henrietta House
9 Henrietta Place
London W1M 9AG

Age Concern
Bernard Sunley House
60 Pitcairn Road
Mitcham
Surrey

Employment Fellowship
T H Oakman OBE JP (Director)
Drayton House
Gordon Street
London WC1 0BE

The London Voluntary Service Council
68 Charlton Street
London NW1

National Council for the Single Woman and her Dependants
Miss Heather McKenzie (Director)
29 Chilworth Mews
London W2 3RG

National Council for Voluntary Organisations
Nicholas Hinton (Director)
26 Bedford Square
London WC1B 3HU

REACH (Retired Executive Action — Clearing House)
Victoria House
Southampton Row
London WC1B 4DH

2 Mental outlook and relationships

The framework

A vital point about successful retirement has already been made: namely that the cornerstone is continued mental and physical stimulation. One fallacy is that the older person inevitably faces a state of gradual mental decay. This is largely nonsense and it is easy to name men and women who go on being successful, creative and active well into their eighties — many even have the motivation to be successful in new fields of endeavour.

Another lie is that old dogs cannot learn new tricks. It has recently been shown, by research carried out at the Max Planck Institute in West Berlin, that 'pensioners' can be taught and have the capacity to acquire new skills and knowledge. Methods of teaching need to be different to provide the right stimulation, and sufficient motivation has to be there because it can be quite hard work but it is nonetheless perfectly possible. Retirement must be accepted as a period of about twenty years which provides the opportunity, and more importantly the challenge, to lead a new and different life. It is a chance to do new things, at a more gradual and less competitive pace, that should provide the stimulus to develop a new role and accept a second but useful and rewarding identity. And of course an individual's past skills and reputation can be exploited. Many people continue in much the same role and this keeps them interested and in circulation. But it is usually more exciting and therefore more stimulating to look for new challenges to broaden your horizons.

There are two further pieces of the stereotype which are more accurate but given insight can be overcome. The first concerns the ability to accept new ideas. It is commonly believed that all great advances in inventive thought are made by youngsters who have an intuitive flash and are prepared to follow it up. This is to a degree what Edward de Bono calls lateral thinking.

The problem is that as we get older we tend to become the slaves of our own experience and what is regarded as the perceived or traditional wisdom in a particular field. Also, of course, we have seen it all before and tend to be reluctant to face the hassle of change. This makes us reactionary and resistant to it. We are comfortable with what we know, understand and are used to. Any sort of change tends to be seen as threatening and to be resisted: all of which is reinforced by our own previous experience.

Thus, older people, unless they are careful to avoid the pitfalls, want to play safe and stay in the comfort of their rut. But this, if uncorrected, is a slippery slope towards minimal activity and is likely to produce decay. By understanding what will happen to your behavioural reactions, and fortified by the reassurance that abilities can be developed, successful retirement involves a willingness to accept the discipline of continued stimulation.

Having too little to do is the main danger to be avoided. Conscious choices have to be made to develop an appropriate retirement life style. The right things seldom just happen. The deprivation of work — a form of bereavement — has to be consciously replaced by new activity. It is the experience of most of us that long before retirement we tend to become more forgetful and fail to remember telephone numbers, shopping lists, etc. Older people worry about this and become afraid that it marks the onset of senility. It does not.

We now know more about how parts of the brain and nervous system function and consequently what causes, and to a degree, can cure, malfunction. The brain seems to be a cross between a computer and a switchboard. Like everything electronic, it gets less efficient as the insulation breaks down and the connections become worn. Also, like an ageing sound reproduction system, there is an increase in background noise or static which does not help efficiency. But on the whole the system goes on working, albeit more slowly. The way in which the memory works is not yet understood but there must be an indexed data bank in which information, or experience, is stored by imprinting. It must obviously be capable of access on demand by certain trigger mechanisms. It is common knowledge that most of us have good long-term memories. We can remember the past and our current reactions are formed by the interplay of personality and past experience. It also seems that as we get older our memory of early life tends to sharpen. But when it comes to remembering a telephone number, or all of three or four shopping items, memory fails in a rather unpredictable way. This is called short-term memory and is better in children than adults, perhaps because they do not have so much to remember and possibly because there is plenty of spare storage space. Clearly, too, this is a protective mechanism because the brain cannot go on remembering everything forever. Such a perfect filing system would have to be of infinite size. Thus short-term memory does fail with age for understandable functional reasons. Imprinting for retention has to be more positive, recall gets less efficient on marginal imprinting and the whole system is rusty because of wear and tear.

All this is normal and should give you no grounds for anxiety. I have found that my short-term memory is subject to fatigue. It is worse at the end of the day and when I am overtired. Part of the art of growing old gracefully and living in a family or other group, without becoming a drag, is to recognise, accept and discount these changes, thus minimising the impression of becoming a doddering old reactionary. Short-term memory is best dealt with by realising that it is prudent to write lists and memos — and then remembering to read them. Avoiding becoming the slave of your past experience or an institutionalised version of your younger self is much more difficult. Much of the change and many of the trends in today's life do not appeal to us older people. But, trite though it may sound, the world has always changed and it will be inherited and developed by the next generation. Strive for tolerance and understanding and be willing to turn off the personal gramophone record except perhaps for your wife, husband or good friends who either agree or regard it as an acceptable price paid for the rest of the relationship.

Another major change that happens with age is the increase in reaction time. This is the speed with which you can respond to changes or stimulae, like a hot kettle handle or a traffic light.

This is probably best seen in car driving, which requires skilled adaptation and response to a rapidly changing situation. Older people, particularly as they drive less, find it increasingly difficult to respond in time. Often the scene has changed, or the opportunity passed to overtake safely. The same is true for being a pedestrian or catching a bus. Again, there is nothing you can do about this but be brave enough, particularly in the case of driving, to stop in time to avoid an accident. I failed to stop both my parents from driving in time to avoid the predictable accidents which terminated their driving. Mercifully these only involved the write-off of two cars: both my parents were then over eighty.

There are two important morals here. The first is that learning can continue and that new challenges must be sought out and met. This is the key to remaining and appearing young and active. The second is that there are inevitable changes and limitations that come with age. They come at different rates and times but by understanding them and making the necessary behavioural corrections, their effects can be considerably mitigated.

I suspect, although it is impossible to prove, that the changes can be delayed by living actively and participating in life. Optimism and involvement are more rewarding than negativity and defeatism. Old dogs must be prepared to learn new tricks to go on surviving pleasurably.

Stress and relaxation

Stress is a popular, misused and badly understood term. Being stressed, or thinking that you are, has to some extent become a cult. Wives, for instance, like to describe their husbands as being stressed and harrassed. Similarly, the busy professional finds it difficult to admit that he is thoroughly relaxed and on top of the job. To be so is perhaps to have failed or be capable of doing more. In my terminology this is not stress.

We all need challenge to keep us going and provide stimulation. Challenge is, in fact, a biological necessity for all living things. Challenge, at various levels in our daily lives, successfully dealt with, is satisfying and exhilarating. It needs to come from a variety of sources but only when the challenge becomes too much do we experience stress.

I think it is important to realise the difference between stress and challenge: the one being essential and desirable and the other being a potentially dangerous manifestation of overload.

The trouble is that the stress reaction, which is biologically defensive, as it were, to get you off the hook, happens at a sub-conscious level and we don't recognise the chain of cause and effect unless we have developed insight. The reactions too are many and various and I believe that they destroy well-being by causing illness, which is why I believe in the holistic approach to analysing the cause and proper treatment of symptoms.

An essential feature of this philosophy is to realise that we function at different levels on a range of networks. You may be good at some things and bad at others, the latter being stress-ful. All this too is very much a function of basic personality and past experience. Not all of us are good at people and relation-ships, and when in senior positions, or in the family, tend to be insensitive to the effect we have on others. We do not see our-selves as stressors, which is both unfair and unnecessarily painful to our associates. Tense, anxious and obsessive people, particularly if they are also introvert perfectionists, will obviously find life more difficult than relaxed extroverts. Although it is difficult to change personality traits, if they are understood it is easier to live with them, both for you and the people around you.

It must also be accepted that under-employment or lack of challenge is just as stressful as too much challenge. This is, of course, what may happen in retirement. The let down of no fixed routine and all the other losses of retirement can be stressful and produce the same sort of depression as is associ-ated with true bereavement, which is why it is essential to have plenty to do and people to relate to in a stimulating way. But if work as one gets older has become stressful, much of this should go with retirement which may then be seen as desirable relief. Tense, anxious people, however, may carry this on into retirement and find it difficult to enjoy their new lives.

Over the past few years there have been significant advances in developing and teaching relaxation techniques and what are called coping skills. These skills are particularly useful for tense executives and professionals of any age because they do help to reduce the strain of coping. They consist of a mixture of developing insight into the events which cause stress, and relaxation to deal with them.

I would recommend anyone, if they are a tense, highly strung worrier, to consider trying one of these techniques. There are several of them, including two sorts of yoga. They do produce tranquillity and also help sleep, and you should now have time to devote an hour or so a day to this. I know many older people who have found their lives much easier once they have learnt to relax and unwind.

There is plenty of literature about relaxation and I would recommend *The Alternative Health Guide* by Inglis and West, published by Michael Joseph. The essence is to find a method and teacher which suits you. Some adult education schedules now include relaxation classes which are well worth trying.

Sleep

Sleep is precious and if you are one of those lucky people who can drop off anywhere at any time, this section is not for you.

Mythology has it that older people sleep less well and dream more disturbingly than younger ones. There is no evidence for this but those who had sleep difficulties tend not to find it any easier, except of course when this is anxiety related and the anxiety is removed by retirement. I suspect that part of the mythology stems from two sources: lack of exercise and boredom. It is a truism but you do have to be tired in order to sleep or, put the other way round, it is hard to stay awake if you are physically tired. And doing nothing much all day, possibly eating too much as well, is not conducive to the relaxed tranquillity that going to sleep requires. A good flat bed with a hard mattress is desirable and the probability is that the bed you got married in, is not the one in which to die. If one partner sleeps less well or wriggles about, don't be too proud, separate beds may be a solution.

Warmth and comfort are obviously important to sleep and I have found that an electric over-blanket, preferably a double one with dual controls, is an admirable modern convenience for better sleep. In my view, too, the open window has no place for the elderly. There are usually only two cures for snoring: ear plugs or separate rooms. I believe that there is a place for sleeping pills although they are currently out of medical fashion: worth discussing with your doctor.

Much research has been done about sleep and sleep rhythms and it does not seem to matter much as to whether you get all your sleep at night or take some during the day. Individual sleep needs vary from five to eight hours and if it suits you, there is a case for a regular afternoon nap rather than getting all your sleep at night. Retirement is about doing what you want when you want. There is everything to be said for getting up at five, if you are awake then, and sleeping during the day. If you tend to drop off after supper and live with a younger family, a nap may make you less anti-social in the evenings.

You may also have found, in the few years before retirement, that you tire more easily and don't have the ability for sustained endeavour. This is a normal age effect and may be, to some extent, related to lack of exercise. As I got older I found that it took me much longer to recover if I became overtired. This again is due to age, anxiety and a degree of boredom with work. You have seen it all before. It is a good idea to be careful not to get overtired and irritable. Watch out for this and ask your spouse to and then take a break or get some extra sleep and relaxation. I suspect, too, that if you are actively involved there is a case for three or four breaks a year. They need not all be long ones. Fatigue is the enemy of enjoyment and well-being is the antidote to disease.

General tension and anxiety do make sleep difficult because although the muscles are still, the mind races and worries, usually in unproductive circles. Tense, perfectionist and obsessional people can't shrug these characteristics off in retirement. If you are like this, it may well be that here too a relaxation regime, of which there are now plenty about, will be helpful. They all depend on a trick or gimmick, which is fine. The problem is to find the one to suit you and offered by a convincing teacher with whom you have rapport. Early retirement is a good time to experiment in relaxation.

Relationships

When, twenty-five years ago at the Institute of Directors, I started to try to understand the health, rather than the disease problems of the members, I became inevitably involved in the emerging field of stress and what was then called psychosomatic medicine. This meant learning about the life style and pressures to which my patients were exposed. We soon realised that there were three main environments: work, home and leisure. This last is particularly important from middle age onwards and it is sensible to get pleasure and relaxation from totally different activities. In fact it is the antidote to workaholism from which so many of my patients suffered and which made them both vulnerable and boring people. They had no outside interests. It also became clear that nearly as much stress arose from domestic as from professional or work sources. The hard driving executive tended to neglect his wife and family, especially if he travelled a great deal. I found, too, and this was in the sixties, that these men often had difficulties with teenage children with whom they really had rather little contact. The problems then became stressful and produced feelings of guilt. As well as this we got the impression that many wives had a raw deal. They had had the income and the status but rather little real contact. To a degree this was their fault because they did not insist on a better and more human relationship. The situation has improved since then. Wives are both more demanding and, perhaps more important, increasingly involved in activity outside the home. One of my key questions to a man coming for a health check used to be 'what job satisfaction does your wife get out of being married to you?' Hopefully, if I got the timing right, this led to a rethink of the relationship — which is important in middle age, with the children growing up.

All of this highlights the importance of relationships. These become much more critical in retirement to fill the void created by loss of work and its associations. As a culture or society, I suspect that we are bad at relationships, which may be one of the factors responsible for the relative breakdown of the family and the consequent loneliness of the 'abandoned' elderly.

Some of this may be due to English reserve — the stiff upper lip and all that — plus an unwillingness and lack of tradition in discussing problems and difficulties openly and honestly. We also find it hard to treat our children as adults and rather expect them to continue in the childhood 'dependent . . . obedient . . . grateful' role. This makes them regard their parents as a duty and not a pleasure and may therefore limit contact with grandchildren. This is a pity because grandchildren can be precious in retirement and grandparents in their role can be very valuable to their children. But sadly grandmothers, particularly, can cause friction and tension by disapproving of the way in which the grandchildren are being brought up and trained. Some of this may be legitimate but much of it stems from the generation gap, grandparents tending to expect that the way in which children should be brought up is static, remaining the same as it was in their day.

A marriage that has rubbed along reasonably well at a rather superficial level, is often put under strain by much greater contact and perhaps an element of boredom. This can be made worse by a change of residence to a new area without an adequate social network. It is, perhaps, more difficult for a person whose life centres around the home to establish a new identity and they may become isolated and fractious.

This is not the forum to explore the problem in greater depth but I want to make the point and a plea for the need to rethink relationships. In some retirement seminars I have managed to develop useful discussions about relationships and to get couples to discuss, objectively and without acrimony, some of the quirks of their spouses that irritate them. If you are going to embark on the next twenty years of productive tranquillity, it could be sensible and useful, as it were, to have it out and start again. I think that there is a case for what might become a second honeymoon to start this off. There is also the problem of possible role change: the husband now has more time at home and need not be looked after so much. There is in fact every reason for encouraging him to look after himself and share the chores much more. It may be that a neutral counsellor, good friend or professional will help to get the dialogue going and keep the temperature down. There is nothing to be gained by starting a slanging match but much by becoming more open in discussing problems.

Another area requiring openness is the problem of planning what will happen when one of you dies, and usually it will be the man who goes first. Do you both know about wills, solicitors, executors and so on? Do you know how much money there will be and how immediately available it is? It is quite extraordinary, in otherwise seemingly responsible people, how little many wives know about what will happen to them when they are left on their own.

It is much easier to do all this before it becomes an acute problem and it is a legitimate area for family discussion, so that everyone will at least have a rough idea of a contingency plan. This will reduce some of the shock of bereavement and facilitate the inevitable readjustments. Death comes to all of us and it is sensible to know what we want to do about it.

The British are bad at bereavement, perhaps because it is badly handled by doctors and nurses, but also because our national reserve inhibits the expression of grief and friends are frightened to talk to us. Grieving is a natural and necessary process and unless it is encouraged, the process is halted and the survivors never re-emerge into reasonable social life. They remain bottled up with their memories and guilts. It is a good exercise and socially valuable to make a point of supporting any friend or relative who has been bereaved. If you talk to them afterwards, many will say that once the funeral was over nobody wanted to know them, largely because their friends were too embarrassed to talk through the situation.

The last area about which I have strong views is the question of discussing the possibility of death. If someone is dying of cancer, it is obvious to both the sufferer and the family. But how often do they all, encouraged by the doctors, pretend that recovery is still round the corner. Do make a point, now before it happens, that you want to know the truth about any illness and face up to it together and as a family. It may sound trite and patronising but I can claim that families who are quite open about what is likely to happen, at any age, and who share the whole experience are enriched by it. The sadness is easier to bear.

People do need people and we all need to be wanted. Relationships are most of what is left as we get older. In our society they seem to me to need better cultivation than they often get. This should not be too difficult for mature people.

Sex after sixty

It is difficult to write usefully in detail about sexual activity in older people. This is because of the wide, and completely normal, range of variation in both need and performance. But I think that it is fair to make the point that for most couples sex becomes less important in later life.

What is important, however, and this is probably the most important point in this section, is that couples should continue to express their affection in a physical way. Even if there is no complete intercourse, there can still be plenty of physical contact and conscious effort made to show that love and affection are fully maintained. It is a help if you do things for each other, show appreciation and don't take it all for granted.

Inherently there is no reason why sexual intercourse should stop until after seventy but folklore has it that it should. This is nonsense. The Victorian attitude that intercourse is something that should be confined to the reproductive phase is finally dying. Women should find the menopause liberating because the risk of pregnancy is no longer present and precautions do not have to be taken. In fact it can be a period of mild abandon. Any menopausal problems should be dealt with, if necessary by attending a special clinic. Today there is no excuse for tolerating severe symptoms for months or even years. It is hard on women that most doctors are men, many of whom remain in the 'grin and bear it' era of non-intervention.

A main problem for women is that there may be some vaginal dryness after the menopause but this is easily dealt with by a simple lubricant jelly or even a hormone cream. Here a doctor or clinic should help with advice.

Sexual performance and need in older people tends to be determined, firstly, by past performance and, secondly, by regularity. Those who may only have intercourse about once a month will tail off and find it more difficult than if it happens once a week or so. It will usually be found that stimulation and arousal take longer but this should make it more fun.

It is also sensible to stop the event falling into too set a pattern, as it tends to do without thought. New approaches should be tried and different times of day, or even different places, may help. Fatigue is the enemy of libido and as the run up to retirement is often a period of stress and fatigue, sex does tend to run down, leading to a feeling that this is the end of the sexual road. Again, this is not inevitable and a honeymoon atmosphere plus an increase in general well-being should reverse the trend. Difficulty tends to arise when the needs and abilities of you both begin to go in different directions and rather than doing anything about it, the situation is left to drift into one of no attempt and no success: plus a certain amount of guilt.

Men particularly may find it more of a problem to become aroused and then begin to feel guilty. Anxiety builds up and a vicious circle sets in. In spite of what the advertisements say, there are no magic remedies and on the whole drugs and potions fail to help in the long term. However, there may be a short-term placebo effect.

If the woman finds intercourse uncomfortable there is probably a physical reason and your doctor or a specialist should be consulted. The cause is nearly always simply dealt with. The main thing is to overcome any reluctance to seek advice. It is normal, reasonable and desirable to continue enjoying your sex life.

Should there be problems or difficulties, two steps can be taken. The most important is to be frank and open about them so that friendly discussion and understanding of each other's problems and needs will lead to a new and more satisfying regime. If this fails, or if a neutral counsellor would help to break the ice, it is worth pursuing this line. This is a relatively new area of expertise and your doctor, the Family Planning Association or Marriage Guidance Council will give advice on who to consult. Whoever you go to will certainly want to see both of you, separately and together. You should not give up without a good honest try to get going again. Much of what you do and your attitude to it needs reappraisal and discussion in retirement. Your sex life is no exception to this but you may need to be brave to get it sorted out. Given the right approach and a high sense of well-being, this should not be difficult.

3 Keeping physically fit

I have recently completed a fascinating exercise on fifty volunteers who, in groups of ten, were offered six months supervision at five Fitness For Industry centres in various parts of the country. Their ages varied from fifty-seven to seventy-two with most of them well over sixty. None was fit beforehand and several had medical disabilities, such as high blood pressure or moderate angina. One man had an artificial leg. The regime was moderately arduous and the early stages required much determination to continue because of the aches and pains.

The object was to measure physical improvement and also get some idea as to its possible benefits. Virtually all of them, men and women, showed measurable improvement in strength, pulse rate, oxygen utilisation and, in some cases, reduction in blood pressure. They all felt significantly better and more lively, and several lost many of their previous aches and pains. Most of the people promised to keep it up in one way or another, but the most impressive factor was that they all felt so much better and were able to do more in the rest of their day. Each group also developed great supportive solidarity and the operation developed into a social support group, perhaps partly replacing the loss of association with work. In medical terms, we also demonstrated significant improvement in symptoms like angina or a reduction in drugs required. Most people slept better.

It is difficult to prove statistically a relationship between physical fitness, well-being and effectiveness, but it is reasonable to assume that this exists for most of us. Rare beings will proclaim that they survive because they lie down when activity is mooted but for most of us reasonable physical fitness, particularly as one gets older, is a sensible discipline. In physiological terms, muscles exist to be used and joints to be regularly flexed. Without this, joints creak like a rusty gate with unused hinges and muscles become flabby. It is easier to keep up muscle strength by regular use than to restore weakness that has been acquired by disease and disuse. This means that about half an hour a day, as a minimum, should be spent taking brisk exercise (even going up and down stairs in a block of flats in bad weather). The heart muscle comes in to this. It too has to be kept fit and have a reserve by being made to cope with getting out of breath. This is why patients who have had a coronary thrombosis or heart operation are now sent to a supervised gymnasium.

One of the stereotypes of getting older is that one becomes weaker. This is largely untrue, you can go on being strong if you use your muscles regularly. What is required is two separate regimes: the first to maintain mobility and flexibility by bending and stretching exercise; the second to develop and then maintain strength by aerobic exercise producing mild breathlessness. There is no ideal way to do this. Anything is better than nothing and it is never too late to start. In spite of what some doctors say, there are few medical disabilities that preclude some sort of exercise. The words 'you are getting older, you must take it easy' should be banned from medical parlance. Your body will tell you when it has had enough and if you do a little more every day it is surprising, and encouraging, how much you improve.

The important thing is to do what you enjoy most or dislike least: walking, jogging, dancing, swimming, gardening and so on. There is also an increasing number of fitness centres which offer supervision and encouragement with special sessions for retired people. Swimming, if available, is good for older people because it is non-weight bearing and uses all the muscle groups.

I have purposely not gone into details of exercise and fitness schedules because there are so many available. I would, however, mention the *BUPA Book of Fitness and Wellbeing* published by Macdonalds (October 1984). This gives details of individual exercises and a range of aerobic activities and sports. Each section is age and sex rated so that anyone can slot themselves into a regime. As the editor, I say with due modesty that much in this book will help and encourage older people to live sensibly.

Included in any fitness exhortation is the question of weight. Life insurance companies discovered many years ago that thin people live longer than fat ones. More important in later life is the simple fact that the less there is of you to cart around, the easier it is. Equally if there is a bit of arthritis, bad back, hip or knee, it is essential to minimise the load on this, by weight reduction. In spite of disability it is essential to keep mobile.

Reasonable physical fitness has five benefits:

- you are likely to live longer
- you will feel better
- you will perform better and have more general energy
- you will feel virtuous about it and, provided you don't become a bore, it is legitimate
- you will sleep better.

It is never too late to start and there is always room for improvement.

Arthritis, rheumatism and mobility

Rheumatism is a diagnosis beloved by doctors and accepted by patients. Used loosely, it refers to a non-existent disease but becomes a useful dumping ground for the various aches, pains and twinges that beset us all. These have a multitude of real and imagined causes and it is not the purpose of this section to go into them in detail except to say that any cure that works is legitimate. Fringe treatments like osteopathy, manipulation, acupuncture and so on may well be better than 'proper' medicine.

Rheumatoid arthritis, on the other hand, is very much a disease, involving inflammation of the tissues around joints and destruction of the joints themselves. It is a destructive disease, tending to be more common in women. Its cause is unknown and there is a range of treatments, some of which work some of the time. I believe it to have a large stress element but not everyone will agree. It is dealt with by rheumatologists.

Rehabilitation from injury, disability and strokes, as well as rheumatoid arthritis, is dealt with by specialists in physical medicine, who are not always the same as rheumatologists, and physiotherapists. Orthopaedic specialists are surgeon carpenters who deal with injury, deformity and bone disease. Clearly there is some overlap in these three groups and neurosurgeons also get in on the act when nerves are involved — as they often are in prolapsed discs.

Osteo-arthritis, or arthritis for short, is a wear-and-tear disease of joints in which the protective cartilage over bone ends gets eroded and pain results. It also follows injury or infection. Obviously it is more common in older people, worse in the overweight and may result from overload or compensation. Thus, a bad back, old knee injury or a short leg, leading to years of compensation to get both feet on the ground or keep your head straight, puts a strain on other muscles and joints which finally rebel and become painful and arthritic.

It is also a fact of physiology that if a joint, like the knee, becomes injured or swollen, the muscles surrounding it become weak because the pain stops them being used. A vicious circle is set up because weak muscles lead to more injury. This is particularly true of back pain when an original injury, perhaps treated by a corset or brace, leads to weak muscles. The back then becomes vulnerable and continues to be over-protected, creating another vicious circle. It is therefore essential to keep up muscle strength by regular special exercises to maintain tone and mobility.

There is another point related to mobility and that is the danger to older people of falling over. When I worked in a busy casualty department after the war we used to know that on a slippery night we would get our quota of broken wrists and hips. Bones, particularly in women, become more brittle with age and hence more fragile. The sense of balance and ability to react quickly also diminish. If you do have a mobility problem or it is slippery, don't be too proud to use a stick, which can be the greatest help. It must be strong enough, have a good handle and a rubber tip. Above all, it must be the right length so that it will take your weight with the arm more or less straight.

To summarise, physical stimulation is essential to maintain liveliness. Muscles and joints must be used regularly in winter and summer to the extent of producing mild breathlessness. Any form of exercise will do but swimming is recommended for older people. Strength only diminishes with age because of disuse. It is never too late to start. Try getting a medium sized dog and take it out yourself. I can promise that the relatively sedentary who get themselves fitter will feel much better. Age is little barrier to many games, if played with peers and not tyros.

Keeping in good trim

Most of the points about maintaining your well-being have already been made and you should have started investing in your health in middle age. I am a strong protagonist of the health check and regard this as preventive maintenance on people. It is like having your car serviced. Early changes can be picked up and dealt with, and life style problems dicussed. It seems to me to be sensible to keep this up although the procedures need not be so extensive as at a BUPA centre. Sadly, the NHS is not prevention oriented but some GPs and group practices do offer simple health checks and if you can afford it one of the specialist centres will be pleased to go on seeing you. It is wise to have hearing, vision, blood pressure, blood and urine checked every year or eighteen months, largely to ensure that there has been no change and that insidious diseases like diabetes have not crept in.

Older people expect to get a bit stiff and less mobile and if they have a long standing disability, like deafness or a bone deformity, they expect it to get worse. Similarly many GPs may label someone a diabetic or whatever and tend not to look for other conditions. I think it wise to seek expert advice every two or three years about any disability. After all, the state of the art may have changed and new treatments become available, so do try to get a regular simple health check.

Warning signs and symptoms

I make the point in the special section for women (see page 63) that you control your own medical destiny. Doctors, sadly, never seek out their patients to see how they are. This is something which they ought to do for their older ones. It rests with you, therefore, to report any changes or discuss any anxieties.

Dealing with most diseases, particularly cancer, depends on early diagnosis. This in turn depends on the patient reporting early to the doctor who then has to clutch at straws and make sure that the symptoms are not significant. It is always up to the patient to report to the doctor and not put it off because he does not want to bother him. Doctors are there to be bothered — legitimately and sensibly — and to bother about their patients.

Any change or set of symptoms which lasts for more than a fortnight should be reported. The main changes to look out for are:

- Loss of weight and appetite.
- Great gain in weight without dietary over-indulgence.
- Persistent headache.
- Change in sleep pattern, waking early and feeling gloomy. Depression is common, treatable and often missed. Tranquillisers and sleeping pills do not help.
- Breathlessness, persistent cough and swollen ankles at the end of the day. A mild degree of ankle swelling which has gone by the morning is almost normal.
- Any bleeding from anywhere, from coughing, vomiting, rectum or vagina, must be reported at once.
- Any bleeding or pain from a skin lesion or change in the size or appearance of an established mole or skin blemish: report at once.
- Change of bowel habit or difficulty. This can be looseness or constipation, or alternate. Most bowel cancers present like this, with pain, discharge or discomfort. If caught early they respond well to surgery.
- Any pain anywhere which is new and persists for more than a few days, particularly if it is not related to an injury.
- New lumps or bumps that you can see or feel even if they are painless. 'Old friends' are safe to leave provided they don't change.
- Pain in the leg or chest on walking or exercise.

The list could be endless but these are the main signals. What it adds up to is to be sensible about any new symptoms. Don't hope that they will go away, but get a check on them. Most will turn out to be harmless but it is very much a case of a stitch in time. The onus for threading the needle rests on you.

Diet and digestion

We live at a time when fashion and exhortation about diet is rampant and it must be difficult for the average person to keep a sense of perspective in the face of conflicting advice. There are, however, two main threads running through this tangle.

The first is to keep your weight within reasonable limits, roughly within 10 per cent of optimum. For most people this is purely a matter of calorie book-keeping. If you eat more calories than are required for daily life, these are banked as fat. Thus the overweight person on a steady diet ticks over with a large credit account. Eating is very much a matter of habit, and of family and cultural group behaviour, so that eating patterns tend to be rigid and passed on through the children. Some of us are better converters than others and have to be careful. Others, the thin active ectomorphs, can eat what they like and never put on weight.

The second and more important thread is the need to reduce the toll of coronary heart disease which, although dropping in the USA, is still static and high in this country. Coronary heart disease is multi-factorial in its causes but diet, in particular the fat content, is undoubtedly important. In developed countries the consumption of animal fats and dairy products has increased since the war, so too have the average weights of the population. Obesity has been called the commonest disease and we do all tend to suffer from over-nutrition. For good reasons there is now considerable pressure, supported by the government and their expert advisers, to get back to a more 'natural' diet. This is not organic food, for there is no hard evidence of the benefits of this, but a more fibre-rich diet with fruit, vegetables and wholemeal products and much less meat and dairy products. This does have nutritional advantages but obviously conflicts with the farming lobby and EEC policy. The human digestive system is designed to function on bulk and it does need a good volume of roughage to push through, particularly as it gets older and less flexible.

Another trend, especially for single people and small families, is to be tempted by packaged, convenience foods. Although often tasty, they have, by definition, to be short of fibre or low in residue.

What this boils down to for older people is to eat more or less what you like provided that you keep your weight at a reasonable level. Bearing in mind the need for regular exercise, it is easier to achieve this without having too much weight to cart around. After retirement, the load on an inevitably ageing system, bones, joints, and muscles as well as the heart should be minimised to reduce wear and tear.

I have found over my clinical years that many older people do tend to experience bowel trouble. This is often miraculously improved by a modest increase in fibre — taking bran cereal for breakfast, for example. I believe too that the human engine is designed for regular feeding and likes three meals a day, but they need not be heavy ones. Age on the whole demands simpler food at regular times with plenty of fruit, vegetables and fibre and not too much animal fat.

If you have a digestive problem, perhaps an old ulcer (although these are now much less common), hiatus hernia or difficult colon, it is likely to improve with retirement and lessening tension. The digestive system is particularly prone to stress and anxiety and usually improves on holiday and in retirement. But if this does not happen in, say, three months, you should see your doctor and have it re-investigated.

Fluid intake becomes more important with age. The kidneys function less well and lose some of their power of concentration. This means more dilute urine will be produced which, coupled with a weaker bladder, means getting up at night. This encourages a tendency to cut down on fluids towards the end of the day which is not sensible. Fluid intake should be kept up at about three pints a day and more in hot weather. Mild dehydration, which must be avoided, does throw an increased load on the circulation and may even precipitate a minor stroke. On the whole it does not matter what fluid is taken but tea or coffee with sugar is a high calorie food and so is alcohol. I am strongly in favour of alcohol in moderation and there is no reason to stop it in retirement. In fact, if you are likely to become alcohol dependent, this will probably have happened already — which is a different problem. But I have known people retiring unsuccessfully, ie without thinking through the problems and making sensible plans, to become depressed and start drinking too much. This obviously has to be guarded against.

Many of my patients have found that their alcohol tolerance diminishes as they get older and that suddenly there are certain drinks they can no longer take. Sadly this is probably a function of an ageing digestion and less efficient liver. The liver has to work quite hard dealing with alcohol and the enzyme systems involved work more slowly. Little can be done to help this except to experiment with various drinks, to take them with meals and in a not too concentrated form. Dry Martinis and brandy may sadly be out.

Salt

There is currently a great deal of controversy about the possible role of salt in the causation of high blood pressure. My own feeling is that it will finally be shown to be an important piece of what is a complicated jigsaw. Again, this is a disease which is multi-factorial. There is a growing volume of evidence to suggest that reduction or elimination of salt will reduce raised blood pressure and also the strength of the drugs required to lower it. This is not, however, to say that too much salt in the normal diet caused the condition in the first place, but for some types of hypertension it could have played a part.

Salt has little nutritional value and is taken largely as a matter of taste and habit. We have all become used to food containing a lot of salt. It is also included in most processed food and dressings. When I was last in America visiting a coronary rehabilitation unit, the doctors complained bitterly that there were no regulations requiring the salt content of processed food to be given on the packet and that it was impossible to buy salt-free products.

It does seem that it would be sensible, and no great hardship, if we all got used to using less salt in our diets (and for once there would be no great socio-economic implications). In the meantime, if you have a blood pressure problem your doctor will advise you about how much salt to take and in any case it would be wise to cut down on extra salt.

Retirement is all about enjoyment but with discipline. Eating and drinking are major pleasures and should continue to be indulged. If you retire in reasonable health you are unlikely to be an immediate coronary candidate and need not worry too much about diet, provided your weight is controlled, enough fibre is taken and fluid intake is kept up.

4 Seeing and hearing

Sight

Most of us require glasses for reading some time in middle age. As the eye gets older the lens and its supporting mechanism loses its elasticity. The eye focuses from distance to near sight by relaxing the lens to alter its focal length. Loss of elasticity means that the near point recedes and small print cannot be seen clearly. As people say, 'my arms are not long enough', and the receding print is then too small.

Reading glasses are merely simple plus lenses which magnify the object. It is, however, important to continue having your eyes tested regularly and to have the right glasses. If you do fine work at a distance different from comfortable reading, it is often sensible to get a pair of specific glasses for this activity.

Short-sighted people go through the same age change which means that their near point retreats in the same way. Thus they need less strong concave lenses and may in fact manage without any at all. They tend to think that their eyes are getting better.

Astigmatism is due to irregularity of the surface of the eye giving distorted vision. This does not change much with age so that the same correction has to be built into any reading or other glasses.

What is not so generally realised is that the ageing eye requires much more light to see efficiently. Most domestic lighting tends to be on the dim side and there is a strong case for retirement planning to include a good pool of light, perhaps an anglepoise for each member of the house. For the same reasons it is wise to review the lighting in kitchens and corridors to minimise accidents and increase efficiency. Put a new light over the stove, the sink and the back door. Accidents account for a lot of disability in the elderly.

Cataract, which is a gradually developing opacity in the lens, is common in older people. It is now much easier to deal with, either by removal or a plastic lens implant. If removed, strong glasses are needed to replace the lens itself and here contact lenses can be a help.

Glaucoma is the commonest cause of blindness in older people. It is due to failure of the drainage system within the eye. Pressure builds up and does the eye no good at all. It tends to be a familial condition and can be acute or chronic. Any pain in the eye, sudden frontal headache or vomiting associated with pain, should be reported at once as a medical emergency because a sudden rise in pressure can cause blindness.

Vision is far too precious to take risks with and although eye strain is a myth, it is prudent to get expert advice. Opticians are good at eye testing and prescribing glasses and there is now direct access to them on the NHS. However older people in particular ought to see an eye specialist if there are difficulties not dealt with by simple reading glasses.

If you want more information about eyes and vision, there is an admirable book, *Eyes — Their Problems and Treatments* by Dr Michael Glasspool, published in the Martin Dunitz Positive Health Series (in fact, the whole series is an excellent source of medical and health information).

Hearing

Although age-related sight changes are accepted and understood and glasses are socially acceptable, it is not generally realised that hearing deteriorates in the same way. The problem is therefore dealt with at some length here, by reproducing — with kind permission of the authors and publisher — two excellent articles on hearing and, specifically, tinnitus, by Dafydd Stephens and Lorraine Jeffrey Nicol of the Audiology Centre, Royal National Throat, Nose and Ear Hospital in London.

Better hearing for the elderly

by Dafydd Stephens and Lorraine Jeffrey Nicol

Introduction

Recent studies by the Medical Research Council's Institute of Hearing Research have shown that about one in four of the adult population of this country complain of hearing difficulties and one in six have significant noises in their ears. The likelihood of having hearing difficulties increases markedly with age, so that only four per cent of twenty year olds have hearing problems, whereas twenty-five per cent of seventy year olds have such difficulties, the percentage increasing in even older people.

A somewhat similar pattern occurs with noises in the ears (or tinnitus), some six per cent of people aged about twenty years having this problem and fifteen per cent of those aged about seventy. A further important fact concerning hearing loss is that mild to moderate hearing losses are far more common than severe losses. Complete deafness is very rare amongst those not born deaf and the average elderly person with hearing problems is generally only moderately hard of hearing.

One of the problems, and perhaps blessings, of most hearing loss in middle aged and elderly people is that it comes on very gradually, causing insidiously increasing difficulties. Consequently an individual suffering from a hearing loss may not be aware that they are having problems, until perhaps someone draws attention to the fact that they:

- no longer hear the telephone and/or doorbell every time they ring;
- need to have the volume of the television or radio at a level which others may find either uncomfortable or annoying; and
- are unable to follow a group conversation with ease.

The gradual onset of hearing loss is only partly responsible for individuals attending an audiology centre for the first time having experienced difficulties for some fifteen years. A further contributory factor is that some of the 'deaf is daft' myth still persists and fuels the social stigma associated with hearing loss and hearing aids.

It is very important to act on your hearing problems as soon as you begin to experience them; a delay in doing so can result in increased difficulties in handling a hearing aid and learning new listening skills. The handling problems may be related to arthritis, stroke, tremor (shaking) or loss of sensitivity in the fingers. The likelihood of someone having any of these problems increases markedly with age. In a recent study on handling skills of people fitted with hearing aids, we found that none of those first fitted in their sixties had serious problems. However, among those fitted for the first time in their eighties, only a third had no real problems. Furthermore, certain causes of hearing loss may be reversible if treated early but are certainly not if left a long time. The importance of acting quickly cannot be stressed enough. Indeed, would you wait fifteen years from the time you begin to have difficulty reading a newspaper before going to visit an optician or ophthalmologist?

What to do if you have hearing problems

What steps then should you take if and when you begin to experience hearing problems and/or persistent or recurrent noises in the ears?

First, you should take advice from your GP. He or she should be able to define whether or not your hearing problems/noises are due to a reasonably treatable condition, whether they could possibly be related to something sinister (very rarely) or whether you require rehabilitative help. In the vast majority of cases, your GP would generally take further advice from an audiological physician or ENT surgeon, except in those whose problems are due to easily treatable causes. In addition, under the present organisation of the NHS, most of the hearing rehabilitative services are based in the hospitals where such specialists are found.

In such a centre, you will probably find that there is no medical/surgical treatment for your difficulties and what you will need is appropriate rehabilitation. While hearing aids will generally play a central role in such rehabilitation, as they constitute the only reasonable form of wearable amplification, there are additional and alternative approaches to helping with certain of the problems arising from hearing loss. The rehabilitative process should be orientated towards solving the problems (disabilities and handicaps) arising from your hearing loss, rather than trying to match a hearing aid to the hearing loss measure. Indeed, in most cases of hearing loss a hearing aid will never restore 'normal' hearing because of the damage to the inner ear (the most common site of hearing loss) resulting in a variety of distortions which cannot be overcome by current electronic technology.

This said, it is important to repeat that hearing aids play a unique part in the rehabilitative process, particularly in communication situations.

Hearing aids

Staying for a moment with hearing aids, it is worth considering the various types currently available. Within the NHS, there is now quite a comprehensive range of behind-the-ear hearing aids, several body-worn aids and a few ear trumpets which still have a limited but useful role. In addition, there are spectacle adaptors for many of the behind-the-ear aids so that, with the aid of your optician, they may be fitted to spectacle frames. This is obviously relevant if you wear one pair of spectacles all the time.

Everyone will have seen advertisements in the popular press for in-the-ear and in-the-canal hearing aids aimed at the need felt by many people to hide their hearing loss and hearing aid. Some of these aids made and fitted by reputable companies do have undoubted acoustical as well as cosmetic advantages. The major drawback of these devices, apart from the fact that they are not normally available on the NHS, is that their controls are very small and difficult to handle for many elderly people, and they may be difficult for them to fit into their ears. Furthermore, most of those currently produced are made, as far as that is possible, to match the individual's hearing loss, so that it is difficult to change their characteristics as the listener adapts to his or her new listening situation or as their hearing changes.

Certain advertisements for 'hearing correctors' with no electronics are frankly misleading. Their only role is in those people with floppy ear canals which are held open by such devices. This is a rare cause of significant hearing loss and the benefit which most people can obtain from such devices is nil.

In the choice or acceptance of any hearing aid or aids it is essential that you, the user, should be able to handle the controls adequately, change the batteries without any problem and fit the earmould into your ear. This last is one of the commonest causes of difficulty among the elderly and it is important that you should ensure that the person fitting the hearing aid gives you adequate training and practice at such fitting. If, after much demonstration and practice, it still proves to be impossible, alternative approaches to wearable amplification should be considered. These include using the hearing aid with a stetoclip, as used by tape typists, or possibly using a device recently come onto the market for less than £20 — a 'listening aid' based on a walkman type amplifier with two-directional microphones going to a stereo headset.

Other aids to hearing

For many people who can manage well in the communication situations which they encounter in their daily life, but have other particular difficulties, so called 'environmental aids' may be more useful than hearing aids. These may also be used to supplement hearing aids in those people who use the latter.

Environmental aids are not provided through the NHS but may be obtained from the Social Service Departments by people who register with them as 'hard of hearing'. Unfortunately, provisions throughout the country are somewhat variable due to the fact that they come under the non-mandatory provisions of the Chronically Sick and Disabled Persons Act.

Environmental aids may be divided into those which provide additional or alternative amplification, and those which provide alerting and warning signals. A variety of such devices was described in the *Which?* magazine, October 1981, and also in various leaflets produced by the Royal National Institute for the Deaf (RNID), 105 Gower Street, London WC1. The RNID also produces a regular newsletter, *Soundbarrier*, full of news on these and other items, together with many helpful articles.

The additional amplification may be applied to telephones, with amplifying headsets, couplers to link them to hearing aids, inductaphones built into the telephone for the same purpose, and additional receivers. A variety of additional amplifier devices is available for television and radio listening with personalised headsets, additional loudspeakers, loop systems and the like.

Alert and warning devices help with problems in hearing the doorbell and the telephone bell when you are not close to them. These may range from extension bells or extra loud bells to systems which flash the lights on and off. A variety of devices are also available for replacing the quiet alarm clock with extra loud systems, flashing light devices or vibrators under the pillow.

In all cases, it is important to consult your Social Service Department or the RNID first, even if you intend to buy such devices yourself, as they can advise you as to what is most appropriate for your needs. In addition, an increasing number of audiology and hearing aid departments have displays of such devices and, in particular, the hearing therapists there (if you have one in your area) usually have knowledge and experience of them.

In many places, hearing therapists or other health care professionals organise communication training, which may be on an individual or group basis. This covers both hearing tactics, lipreading skills, listening skills and advice with other problems.

Lipreading classes or groups may be useful as long as you do not expect them to transform you from a hopeless lipreader into an expert. The chances are, indeed, that you are already a good lipreader without being aware of it. The real importance of such groups is that you can learn much from how other people have overcome their hearing problems, come to realise that you are not alone with your difficulties, and learn many ways in which you can make communication easier for yourself.

Conclusions

Overall, the main point is not to be ashamed of your hearing difficulty; it is very common and you should not try to hide it. Indeed, a major hearing aid manufacturer produced a very good poster which said 'Hearing aids are less conspicuous than poor hearing'. Do not pretend that you can hear. You cannot fool most people. Consult your doctor as soon as you are aware of persistent hearing problems, even if only in one ear, and obtain appropriate professional advice to help you deal with the problem from audiology/ENT centres and from your Social Services. If you have difficulties which are not helped by the available aids, be sure to consult the RNID to make sure that there are no devices to make life easier for you and your family. Modern electronics can work near magic.

Once you have done this, you may find that some of the local facilities are inadequate, in health and social service provisions, in places of entertainment and in places of work. It is only by drawing this to the attention of the people responsible, and if they are unable to do anything about it, bringing in your local councillors and MPs, that such provisions will be improved.

Tinnitus

by Dafydd Stephens and Lorraine Jeffrey Nicol

Introduction

Tinnitus is the sensation of sound/s in the ear, ears or head in the absence of external sounds. In most cases this is heard only by the individual concerned, but in a few rare cases, using listening tubes or electronic systems, other people may be able to hear the tinnitus. The sound or sounds heard may be of all types, ringing, whistling, churring, hissing or a great variety of complex sounds or combination of sounds. However, if 'normal' individuals are put in a soundproof room for a long period of time, they will all experience tinnitus equivalent to that reported by patients suffering from the symptom.

Tinnitus is a symptom generally indicating some damage to the inner ear or to other parts of the auditory system. It is a very common symptom experienced from time to time by at least one-third of the adult population. Recent studies have shown that about one in six of the adult population experience tinnitus lasting more than a few minutes. However, only about one in twenty-five of the adult population find it annoying and one per cent or less are seriously disturbed by it. Tinnitus is generally associated with some hearing loss, and because the occurrence of hearing loss increases dramatically with age, the

likelihood of anyone experiencing tinnitus also increases significantly in the elderly.

What should you do if you have tinnitus?

If the tinnitus persists more than a few days, especially if it is
occurring in one ear, you should consult your general practitioner about it. It commonly occurs after fevers, such as
influenza, after exposure to loud noises, with impacted wax in
the ear and in certain middle ear conditions. These generally
tend to settle by themselves or may be treatable by your
general practitioner or by an appropriate specialist.

It is, however, worth mentioning that those who have been
exposed to considerable noise at work, in the armed forces or
otherwise, are much more likely to suffer from tinnitus subsequently than those who have not been exposed to such
noise. It is therefore advisable, if you use power tools for DIY
activities, to use some kind of hearing protection such as ear-
plugs or ear muffs as a preventative measure.

If your tinnitus does not settle by itself or with this treatment,
your GP will refer you to an audiological physician or ENT surgeon who will have the facilities to investigate your problem
further and arrange appropriate treatment of the underlying
cause if it is amenable to such treatment.

It must, however, be emphasised that in many individuals,
either the cause of the tinnitus has been in the past, such as
noise exposure, head injury or a hereditary condition, so that
there is no continuing condition to be treated or, alternatively,
it is impossible to identify a cause despite extensive investigation. In this case, the specialist must turn to symptomatic
treatment.

Symptomatic treatment of tinnitus

First, it must be stated that there is no universal 'cure' for tinnitus. Most treatments are aimed at helping the patient to accept
and get used to the symptom and to relieve the problems
secondary to the tinnitus, such as sleep disturbance, anxiety,
depression and listening difficulties.

We all tend to imagine that any symptom is an indication of sinister disease, and adequate investigation to provide reassur-

ance helps us to accept any persistent symptom much more easily. Excessive anxiety will tend to enhance the symptom and if the individual ceases to be frightened, this in itself will be therapeutic. Indeed, the normal process with people suffering from tinnitus is to learn to accept their tinnitus and to cease to worry about it although this may take a different length of time for different people and with different patterns of tinnitus.

For those who have difficulties in getting used to their tinnitus, there are three main lines of approach — psychological, acoustical and pharmacological — with more drastic and destructive approaches such as surgery being restricted to the more severe cases, resistant to all other approaches.

Acoustical management

In the majority of people with tinnitus who also have a hearing loss, the first line of approach should be to help their hearing loss with a hearing aid. These have a threefold effect, reducing the amount that the individual has to strain to hear and hence strain to hear through his tinnitus; masking or blotting out the tinnitus with external sounds; and introducing extraneous sounds which distract the individual from his tinnitus. This may be supplemented by introducing more distracting sounds into the most quiet environments, for example, the bedroom such as by replacing the digital alarm clock with a noisy, old-fashioned clock. This approach is valuable for most sufferers. If it results in insufficient masking or distraction, it may be worth trying a tinnitus masker. This is basically a noise generator built into a hearing aid case, which produces a sound which masks out the tinnitus, provides a relief from the particular sound of the tinnitus and puts the loudness of the sound going into the individual's ears under his own control. Many patients find these invaluable but in others they are less effective.

Psychological management

The theory behind this is to stop the individual worrying about his tinnitus and to help him to learn to live with it. Various techniques have been used, including biofeedback, relaxation training and cognitive therapy, with good results. They lead to a reduction in the annoyance caused by the tinnitus but not in its loudness. Such an approach may also have a dramatic effect on the secondary symptoms provoked by the tinnitus.

Pharmacological management

Only one drug, Lignocaine, has been shown to be consistently effective in actually suppressing tinnitus in a majority of sufferers, but unfortunately that can only be taken by injection into the veins, and even then the effect usually lasts only a few minutes. Much research is taking place to find more effective equivalents which can be taken by mouth, but at the moment there is no dramatic cure.

Other drugs may be used to overcome some of the problems which some individuals may have secondary to the tinnitus, such as difficulties in getting to sleep, early waking, depression and general tenseness. These are the drugs used for such conditions in other more general circumstances.

Conclusions

Tinnitus is a very common symptom and is due to a variety of causes, many of which are not amenable to simple treatment. The normal situation is that sufferers get to accept their tinnitus. Should such acceptance not occur, despite reassurance, a variety of psychological, acoustical and pharmacological approaches are available for use, individually or in combination, which can help this process in the majority of sufferers. There is no magical cure for the symptom.

Teeth

by K J Lewis, FDS

A major part of the preventative philosophy that has grown within the dental profession over the past twenty years is that teeth should be saved whenever possible. Since most tooth extractions are for patients in their forties and fifties, the benefits for the over forties are self evident.

More teeth are extracted as a result of gum disease than because of dental decay. Because of new techniques and materials, today's dental surgeon has a wide range of options to transform even the most painful and hopeless looking 'shells' of what were once recognisable teeth, into comfortable and functional teeth again; indistinguishable from the originals, provided that the gums themselves and — more important — the underlying *bone* are adequate to support them.

Let us backtrack a decade or so and consider what kind of problems are being faced by the average fifty year old today. First, you will probably have teeth, and many of them. These teeth arrived in the mouth soon after the NHS was getting under way, so in a sense they were luckier than they might have been had their owner been born ten or fifteen years earlier. The familiar story is that they received, first, some small fillings, and later these were replaced by larger fillings and then a succession of progressively larger fillings over the years until you wonder whether it is only the dentist's willpower that's holding them together. More extensively repaired teeth may have been graced by inlays, crowns or bridges. Some of the teeth may be a little looser in their sockets than they were, or painful to bite hard upon. The gums may bleed when you brush your teeth, or the gums may have receded round the necks of the teeth, exposing sensitive root tissue. If the very thought of a mouthful of ice-cream sends you skywards, or perhaps even the physical act of toothbrushing is painful in these areas, take heart because such problems are usually manageable. It is important to recognise the warning signs, seek professional advice from a dental surgeon and take stock of the situation.

Whatever your age, reflect on the state of your mouth ten years ago, five years ago, two years ago and today. Are things pretty much as they were or are you going downhill fast? Have you lost any teeth over this period? Have you had a succession of problems with specific teeth, and have these been satisfactor- ily resolved? Has your dentist expressed any kind of doubt as to the long-term survival of your remaining teeth, or given you any general feeling that he is trying to 'let you down slowly' without giving you any specific reason or explanation? Perhaps he is an old friend as well as a trusted professional advisor and the only response you have elicited from him is a silently raised eyebrow of pleasant surprise to see so many gnarled old friends still present at the routine check-up, before you exchange the usual social pleasantries. It is a good friend indeed who can put frankness above friendliness and give you sound professional advice in between the laughing and joking.

What you really need, of course, is an honest opinion of your dental and oral health — where you are now and where you are going. If in doubt, don't be afraid to seek a second opinion either from another dentist in general practice or from a consultant.

It is reasonable to suppose that there will be consultant dental surgeons just as there are consultant gynaecologists, eye specialists or whatever; after all, the mouth is a pretty small place and the teeth but one part of it. Surprisingly, there are no fewer than seven major clinical specialities within dentistry itself, not to mention scores more non-clinical specialities, with consultants for every one of them. A consultant in one branch of dentistry has highly specialised skills often remote from those of another branch of dentistry, and in true medical fashion they have confusing titles. When seeking an opinion you obviously need to approach the correct consultant. The ones that will concern you most are:

(1)   Periodontics/periontology — gums.
(2)   Conservative dentistry — natural teeth, fillings, crowns, bridges etc. This includes endodontics, ie 'root-filling' of teeth.
(3)   Prosthetic dentistry — partial and complete dentures, ie the replacement of missing teeth other than by crowns and bridges etc.
(4)   Restorative dentistry — this is a relatively new and growing group of consultants, who are already consultants in at least one of the above three specialities and whose skill and knowledge will probably encompass all of them anyway. They are thus able to give a broader evaluation.

Most of these consultants are located in the main teaching hospitals and dental schools which are found in the larger cities. In the provinces, the consultant at the local district or general hospital will normally be a consultant in oral and maxillofacial surgery (dealing with complex disorders of the mouth and jaws, tumours, fractures etc) or in orthodontics (straightening children's teeth), neither of which should be what you are looking for, but there are a few exceptions around the country which you should now be able to confirm for yourself.

If you want to keep your teeth, you need to find a general practitioner who shares your ambitions, and preferably one whose philosophy of preventative dentistry encompasses the special problems of the older patient. Many of these focus on maintaining the health of the supporting tissues of the teeth — the gums, the underlying bone and the tissues attaching the tooth root to the bone. Treatment should certainly include plenty of practical advice at regular intervals on how to clean your teeth as thoroughly as possible.

This may sound a little like trying to tell granny how to suck eggs, and indeed it can be an unexpected and embarrassing shock later in life to be sat down by somebody young enough to be your granddaughter and be given a lesson in toothbrushing. Most preventative practices now employ dental hygienists; they have been given particular training in their field and their qualification recognises these special skills in the field of dental hygiene. This includes the scaling and polishing of teeth, with various associated techniques, together with dental health education. They also carry out a range of special preventative procedures for children.

The professional cleaning of teeth (scale and polish) is an undervalued and misunderstood procedure. You may know that scale (also known as *calculus* or *tartar*) forms a hard yellowish film on the surface of the lower front teeth. It develops from the invisible sticky film of bacteria called dental plaque which forms in our mouths all day, every day. Unfortunately, the same layer forms *under* the gum where it is invisible and it is here that it helps to cause gum disease unless removed, by providing a hiding place for more plaque. A scaling that simply removes the obvious deposits above the gum and polishes the teeth so that they feel smooth and shiny has really served little or no useful purpose. A hygienist is not a kind of second-class dentist — instead, he or she has been trained to carry out one small part of the dentist's work to a high degree of skill — an important distinction.

When a hygienist or a dental health educator, another kind of ancillary specialist in the modern dental practice, suggests new and unfamiliar ways of cleaning your teeth it is for a good reason. First, your mouth presents a different kind of cleaning problem every time a new filling, crown, bridge or denture is placed and — more surprisingly, perhaps — the teeth do move within the jaws from year to year and indeed from month to month, presenting new and different problems. It is as illogical to expect one toothbrushing routine to last forever as it is to expect the curtains in one house to fit another. Shapes and sizes are obviously different. Similarly, what is right for one patient can be inappropriate for another. So it is with the teeth and gums, and advice on toothbrushing should be on a continuing personal basis, adjusting to changing circumstances, and certainly not a once-and-for-all litany as many people believe.

There are various techniques such as the strengthening or supporting of the remaining teeth with pins, screws or cast posts, crowns, bridges, splints and precision attachments, but for those readers who may have but a few teeth remaining, or even none at all, I must say a word about dentures.

The simplest form of partial denture is the pink or clear plastic plate, carrying plastic artificial teeth. When you bite on this denture much of the force is transmitted to the gum and soft tissues underneath — tissues which are ill-equipped to tolerate such abuse. While the palate, for example, is well supported on bone and capable of accepting these loads, the gum certainly isn't and this, together with the plaque that plastic dentures tend to harbour, can cause rapid deterioration in the health of the gum beneath them.

Metal 'skeleton' dentures — previously made of stainless steel but now normally chrome-cobalt, are not only stronger, but smaller, lighter and less bulky. They cover much less gum tissue and hence are easier to clean and, most importantly, they are shaped to rest upon the tooth surface, with small clasps carefully positioned to keep the denture in place. The dentist carefully designs these dentures so that when you bite on them selected *teeth* take these biting forces, which is precisely what nature has equipped them to do, thus the gums stay much healthier with this type of denture.

A variation on this theme is overdentures — an old technique now enjoying something of a revival. This usually involves 'root-filling' the roots of various teeth, cutting the remaining teeth down to about gum level and making a denture to sit over the top of them. Such a denture is thus excellently supported and stays in place much better than the conventional full set where no roots remain.

The final option when all the teeth and roots have departed is the full or complete denture. Upper dentures have a head start on lower dentures because of the availability of the palate for support and retention. It is not uncommon to have problems with full dentures, particularly lower ones. Even if you don't, it is prudent to have dentures checked every two or three years to ensure that the underlying tissues are still healthy; dentures can also be relined to improve fit. If you have lost weight, or been ill, it may have affected the shape of your mouth and the fit of your dentures.

If you have an old, worn or battered denture that was basically comfortable before you discarded it, do try to retrieve it because your dentist can use it in a replica technique whereby he recreates the better aspects of the old denture and corrects any faults when producing a new set of dentures which often provide the best in all factors: comfort, fit and appearance.

To summarise, it is becoming the exception rather than the rule to end your days in the same toothless state in which you started them. Modern dentistry is unrecognisable from the days of your childhood, and more people can expect to keep more of their teeth longer and later in life.

Free information on dental matters is available from:
British Dental Health Foundation, 88 Gurnards Avenue, Unit 2, Fishermead, Milton Keynes, Bucks.

5 Special problem areas

Special problems — women

Just as the workaholic man is in my view vulnerable and boring so is the 'pure housewife'. Looking after home and family is splendid and has to be done by someone but when there is only home and less family, I believe it to be an inadequate occupation. Becoming an end in itself, it may be over-protective and inflexible, causing friction and perhaps sourness. I know this is a provocative statement but I think it is a danger area. Everyone should have outside interests and activities and if the stairs don't get swept or the supper occasionally comes from the take-away, so what?

So far I have said nothing about the working wife. She is doing two demanding jobs and to manage these she has to be better organised than her husband. Being a mother may also have to be fitted in, which requires thought and priority. I suspect that, given the right mix, children flourish in this more stimulating environment. But the important point about the situation is that it must make for a different relationship, both emotional and financial. It will certainly be a more independent one and perhaps be the better for it. Much more give and take will be required to establish the ground rules and to agree priorities which don't cause friction or jealousy. There is, too, the danger that work will pull you in different directions with the central relationship becoming less important, particularly if there are no children. All these problems can be faced and generally make for better adjusted people. The working wife will face retirement problems more specifically than her more domestic colleague and these have to be faced in the same way as for the husband.

Difficulties do occur when, as they often are, retirement ages are very different. A younger wife will probably want to go on working after her husband, to get a pension or finish a job she thoroughly enjoys. This may well precipitate role reversal. A similar thing is happening with redundancy and men have to be more flexible. Such difficulties have to be realised well in advance and included in the contingency planning discussions. Women seem to be medically tougher than men if only because they manage to live longer in spite of the alleged hazards and strain of child bearing. The differential seems partially due to the fact that women have a much lower incidence of coronary thrombosis (CHD) in middle life. They also tolerate moderate degrees of raised blood pressure rather better. Perhaps the next few years will show a significant increase in their CHD rate, possibly because more are working and smoking cigarettes. In addition, it is probable that prolonged use of the contraceptive pill may contribute to this. Lifestyle plays a part in mortality statistics and this is shown by the sad and avoidable increase in lung cancer in women over the last ten years. It now more or less equals breast cancer as the commonest 'killer' of late middle aged women.

There are two specific medical problem areas for women. The first is gynaecological and the second concerns the breasts. This is not the place to embark on a detailed description of common gynaecological problems like uterine prolapse, fibroids, bladder troubles and so on. All I want to say is that if you have any symptoms, particularly bleeding, pain or discomfort, take them to your doctor at once. The cause is probably trivial and easily dealt with, but if not, early intervention is the key to cure.

Hysterectomy, removal of the womb, is a relatively common necessity, often for benign tumours or fibroids. It is a satisfactory operation and when properly done and sympathetically handled, should cause no interference with sexual intercourse. As with menopausal symptoms, there may be some dryness, easily dealt with by a simple lubricant jelly.

The menopause usually comes on at around fifty. It carries a vast mythology of symptoms and disabilities, nearly all of which are unnecessary. Many women drift through the 'change' with little discomfort, but if you are bothered by symptoms like hot flushes and so on, see your doctor and get some treatment, if necessary from a menopause clinic, of which there are now many about. The symptoms are due to hormone changes and can largely be controlled by hormone replacement — HRT. The vital thing is not to be put off by doctors who think you should suffer for the mortification of your flesh, but insist on treatment. Your sex life can continue for many years after the menopause. The BUPA Medical Centre has an excellent leaflet on the menopause and the book, *The Change of Life*, by Dr Barbara Evans, is admirable.

Breast cancer is still, sadly, an emotive subject and we still see patients who are too frightened to report lumps in their breast. One in about thirteen women dies of breast cancer every year. The breast, particularly as it ages, is a lumpy organ and it is cheering to note that fewer than a tenth of all lumps prove to be malignant. However, and this is critical, all lumps have to be regarded as suspicious until proved friendly by being looked at under a microscope. Experience over the past few years has shown two important things. The first is that successful treatment depends entirely on the removal of any cancer before it has spread and while it is very small. Secondly, and important from your point of view, is the fact that local excision, without the removal of the whole breast, is usually adequate. The days of extensive and mutilating surgery have largely passed.

Breast cancer is four times as common as cancer of the cervix. Thus, there is four times the case for breast screening for early diagnosis using special X-ray techniques with a small radiation dosage. It is now possible to pick up some tumours before they can be felt. Equally important, however, is self examination, taught at screening and Well Woman clinics. You are in the best position to notice any change and to report it at once. Similarly any bleeding or discharge from the nipple must be followed up, as some cancers begin in the ducts rather than in the breast tissue. I would urge every woman to go for breast screening, particularly when over the age of forty, and go every year. Teach your daughters and granddaughters to learn self examination and keep it up every month for life.

Of course the thought of cancer is frightening and so is the fear of losing a breast or being chopped about, but much worse are the risks of getting disseminated cancer. The problems and risks must be faced and openly discussed. Life without a breast is in fact perfectly tolerable, as is the loss of a leg, given the right attitude and adjustment. I know that it is easy for a man to say this but women doctors say it too. Breasts can be reconstructed by silicone implants, and special bras and bathing costumes are fairly easily obtained. Husbands are mostly sympathetic, or can be encouraged to be, so that once openness has been accepted, adjustment should not be too difficult.

In any case, never, never, neglect any lump in your breast — and if you have been successfully treated, tell all your friends about it. Cancer needs publicity about successful and early treatment if its toll is to be reduced.

The BUPA Medical Centres, of which there are now many well spread around the country, all have facilities for breast screening and there are quite a number of other Well Woman clinics. You should attend for regular screening every year. BUPA also have a good leaflet about breast disease and the Mastectomy Association gives admirable advice and support. Many larger hospitals have mastectomy counsellors to help with the problems of readjustment once you leave hospital.

If you act along the lines I have advocated, you will be playing safe and if you are unlucky enough to get a lump, relatively minor surgery should suffice. But as breast cancer is so common, it must be accepted as a not too unlikely event and dealt with by early treatment. Your life is in your hands and most cases can be treated early quite successfully.

Special problems — men

Men have fewer specific problems than women. The main medical problem is to minimise the chances of having a coronary before retiring. The various risk factors are largely life style related: stress, smoking, weight, exercise and blood fats. These have to be dealt with in middle age.

Apart from this, the only other common problem arises from the prostate. This is a gland on the base of the bladder surrounding its exit, the urethra. It has an irritating habit of enlarging late in life and causing obstruction. Prostate trouble is relatively common, causing difficulty in emptying the bladder, frequency and possibly slight incontinence. These are trying but not serious symptoms. The reason for mentioning them is to make the point that if you get symptoms, have them treated early rather than late. Once enlargement starts it goes on and builds up back pressure on the urinary system. This can do more harm than the enlargement itself and there is the risk of acute obstruction as an emergency, perhaps at a difficult time or when you are away on holiday. Prostatectomy used to be an unpleasant and tedious operation but it is now mostly done through a 'magic telescope' without any cutting. The stay in hospital is usually only a few days. The results are excellent and although it may be necessary to repeat the procedure in a few years because of less extensive removal, this too is easy. The only after effect may be sterility because the ejaculatory ducts which pass through the prostate may be destroyed. But, contrary to popular belief, this does not in any way stop sexual activity which can continue as usual. Sterility at this age should be no hardship.

Cancer of the prostate is one of the commoner cancers in men. It can produce the same symptoms as enlargement and is, on the whole, one of the more controlable cancers, mostly by drugs but sometimes surgery. Quite often too, the patient dies peacefully from some other condition.

In older men, particularly, all urinary symptoms should be investigated as soon as they become noticeable.

6 Accommodation in retirement

by Bill Loving

Bill Loving was the founder-editor of 'Choice' magazine. Now retired, he continues to write and lecture on various aspects of retirement planning

A general note

The retirement home, rather like retirement itself, is a fairly modern invention. As a term, it is not to be solely identified with grouped dwellings for the elderly, which are equipped with alarm systems useful in emergencies. Such dwellings are a form of retirement housing, but make up only one aspect of a many-sided subject.

In the context of this contribution, a retirement home is one which has been designed or adapted to meet the retirement needs of an individual. Retirement these days embraces an age group which reaches from the middle-fifties to the nineties or more. Such a vast range means that there is an enormous variety of people and backgrounds, with persons having quite different ideas on what constitutes for them the most suitable type of retirement abode. Older men and women make up a substantial part of the national community and, like younger ones, differ widely in tastes, health, income, expectations and lifestyle. It therefore follows that there is no one general standard model of a retirement dwelling. It also follows that the term itself can apply to a spacious house as well as to a small flat, or anything between.

For anyone sorting out his housing needs in retirement, there are at least three common factors which apply. The purpose here is to outline these and then, in the following sections, to discuss various options.

Factor one is actually to engage in some hard thinking in advance about the shape, size and location of the retirement home. Such thinking will be coloured to a large extent by what retirement means to a person. On the whole, most people appreciate that retirement can last a long time and that it is a period of life which, in this day and age, far from being a run-down to the grave, can be viewed as a period of positive growth and achievement.

The second factor inevitably brings into play the question: Will the kind of home that is ideal for my retirement in, say, my early sixties, continue to be just as good a proposition in another twenty years' time?

The third factor applies to those sharing a home. Sooner or later there will remain just one survivor of a partnership and, statistically speaking, the odds are that the husband is most likely to pre-decease the wife. What effect should this have on one's planning especially when it is remembered that a home which is perfectly capable of being managed by a couple may become a wearisome and expensive burden to someone left on their own?

How far these points should influence a decision on retirement accommodation is strictly for the individual, but some guidelines may suggest themselves in the rest of the chapter.

Moving or staying?

To move on or to stay put? On the whole, orthodox advice from organisations engaged in the housing field for the elderly, sounds almost a negative note. This is understandable enough because most are dealing with aged people whose health and mobility are on the wane. Even if a move has to be made, the received opinion is that it is better to settle in new quarters in the known and familiar neighbourhood rather than to venture into alien territory.

However, if there is an awareness that an option is to play safe, is there not also room for a touch of optimism?

Planning a retirement home must relate to the needs of the people involved. A prudent couple in their sixties may abandon a large house and an equally large garden for a two-bedroom flat in a sheltered housing scheme on the basis that this is an insurance against reaching the eighties and not then being so spry.

There is an obvious logic on their side, but no more than, say, another pair who decide to remain in a sizeable establishment because it has always been their home. The family may have departed, but the fact that they have reached retirement does not constitute a reason for sacrificing space. These are two extremes, but there are some general pointers that may be worth examining.

Any retirement accommodation should be so arranged that it is easy and convenient to run (this applies, of course, to other households, whatever the age group). If a decision is taken to stay on in the present home, there is a case for seeing how suit-able it is for retirement. Can it be re-arranged in ways that equate with growing older?

There is the perfectly true story of one enthusiast given the task of planning his home for retirement who suggested that one should begin by trying to envisage everything likely to go wrong during later years and then equip the premises accord-ingly.

If, for instance, a long illness or some disability was a likely possibility, was there a downstairs room which could be switched to use as a bedroom? Indeed, were there facilities to live without undue strain on the ground floor?

His list included items such as easy access to garden and house; a kitchen with cupboards within painless reach, and with undemanding equipment and storage; and home heating and insulation of a high standard.

He also favoured lighting of a kind that abolished dark patches; grab rails in the toilet and bathrooms; the installation of taps of the lever variety; a good security system for doors and windows, particularly the front door through which visit-ors could be inspected before admittance; and — back to the garden again — the area planted and laid out in such a way that it was no longer quite so labour-intensive.

A healthy and vigorous person, contemplating his forthcoming retirement, may well blench at the prospect of converting his home into the equivalent of a nursing home for his old age. But without going the whole hog, there is a case for being satisfied that the home can be adapted, even if only on a gradual stage-by-stage basis, to meet changing needs. In a sense, it is all part of the business of standing back, figuratively speaking, and taking a long-term look at this particular area.

A virtue of moving (admittedly few would see it in this light at first) is that one is forced ruthlessly to assess anew the worth of all the bits and pieces that have accumulated during a lifetime of work and family domesticity. Attics and spare rooms are often full of articles stowed away years ago and rarely touched since. In the old home so much lumber is taken for granted and it is sometimes quite a shock to realise when organising a removal, usually into less spacious premises, that there has to be a wholesale clear out.

The discipline of having to perform major surgery on one's possessions is escaped by those who stay put. Yet it can be argued that a large part of the cherished clutter of many years can constitute an unnecessary burden as one grows older. To those who remain anchored in the old neighbourhood is it unreasonable to suggest that as part of the process of preparing the home for retirement they, too, should look anew at their accommodation and all it holds?

Finding a new home

Housing mobility among retired people is still confined to a minority, but it is a large minority, especially among home owners, and present trends indicate that it is increasing. A spur to the rising graph is the development of what could be called two-stage retirement home progress. People who initially settled in a dwelling envisaged as good enough to see them through their retirement, often find as they grow older that it is better to move on to a more suitable abode. The move is not necessarily caused by frailty or infirmity. Quite frequently it stems from the actual experience of some years of retirement and the recognition that the moment has arrived for re-thinking the current position.

In general, most people on retirement move within a radius of thirty or forty miles of their old surroundings. The factors which decide a move to a new area are many and various. Sheer economics could play a major part. Selling a large property and buying a smaller one could release a sizeable amount of capital and also lead to lower maintenance and domestic costs. Successful trading down obviously depends on geography. Selling a house up north and buying one down south is not likely to be financially profitable. In reverse, there could be a windfall. Even shifting out of expensive London into slightly less expensive areas south, east and west of the capital, could mean an addition to one's bank balance.

But economics are not usually the ruling factor in going elsewhere. The family home, chosen because of schools and access to work, may be in an environment which has ceased to appeal. Much is made in the to-move-or-stay debate of the possible isolation and loneliness that may result if one shifts away. But local communities are highly mobile and always changing. The nearness of married sons and daughters and their families, for instance, may be a tug, but offspring often have to move themselves in compliance with the demands of their employment.

In selecting a new location, some suggestions can be made. It is fair to assume that if a person is accustomed to the facilities and amenities of an urban life, it is an elementary precaution to check on what a prospective location may have to offer in this respect. Are there local organisations that can cater for retirement interests? What provision is there for recreation? Is the shopping well sited and, preferably, within easy walking distance? How good (or poor) are the various public services such as libraries, adult education facilities, hospitals, dentists, theatres, restaurants, pubs and clubs?

There is, too, an assessment to be made of road and rail communications. A small test is to imagine living car-less in the area. What will replace the service that a car provides? Local bus services should be studied. If a railway station is within easy distance, this is a plus and better still if it is on a main line.

The test over and with the car again, how accessible is the area to the outside world? Few want to live close to a motorway, but being within reasonable distance of one has much to commend it.

Finally, having to put down fresh roots in a new community is not always the hazardous operation that it is often portrayed as being. It is useful if one already has contacts in the area, but even arriving as a complete newcomer re-settlement need not pose a threat. People who have had to move frequently in the course of their working lives are better at it than others because they learn from experience of the need to reach out and mix.

Interests and hobbies which involve meeting others are helpful—hence the need to check on what a new location has to offer. There also has to be a recognition that the onus is on the fresh arrival to make the first move and to be outgoing. It is not much use sitting at home and waiting for callers.

On the whole, the average person should not find it difficult to cease feeling like a stranger, providing he makes the effort to go a handsome half way.

Life on the level — a flat or bungalow

The point of similarity between a flat and a bungalow is that the accommodation is normally arranged on one floor. Otherwise they are vastly different. A flat, unless it is on the ground floor, has to be reached by stairs, which is an argument for making sure that a lift is installed.

Living on one level is less demanding in basic living terms than occupying a two-storeyed house. Whether or not this is a major requirement depends on the individual and his or her particular retirement needs. All one can do is to present some of the main advantages and disadvantages and leave the decision-making to the person concerned.

As a starter, a flat usually means freedom from the care of a garden. External maintenance is, as a rule, a responsibility included in a service charge which is likely to take care of the cleaning and decorating of halls, stairways and other common areas, care of the grounds and insurance of the buildings as well.

There may be a covenant forbidding the keeping of pets; and for those who like do-it-yourself activities a home workshop, however unambitious, may not be possible. Immediate neighbourhood noise can be an affliction, although decibel intrusion is not just confined to flats.

Flats are mostly leasehold from 99 to 999 years, with the lease-holder paying ground rent. Leases with less than 80 years to run may not be so attractive. Flats tend to be compact, which means that they cost less to run and heat and are not burden-some to look after. The disadvantages could include sheer lack of space. Whether life is lonelier in a flat than in a house is an issue which does not admit of rational discussion. So much depends upon the individual and the pulse of his social and outside life.

As for bungalows they come with a garden and, if detached, with a moderately broad strip of ground. Like flats, well-designed bungalows make for efficiency in running. Intelligent planning of the garden, with patio, paving and other landscap-ing can be introduced to save labour. Once more this can be a gradual process. The man who likes a fine stretch of lawn, a display of annuals, a kitchen garden and a greenhouse, can lessen the chores as he thinks fit.

It is always worth mentioning that flats or bungalows fre-quently offer accommodation suitable for a couple, but which may prove cramped when visitors come to stay, particularly married offspring with children. The adequate accommodation of such welcome guests, if calculated in the number of spare bedrooms required, might logically preclude a move to a smaller home. Here, priorities have to be sorted out. A couple seeking a retirement home are wise to consider their own housing needs before anything else. After all, sons and daughters and grandchildren can usually be 'squeezed in' on short stays and to plan otherwise is to acquire accommodation that may be grossly under-used.

Mobile homes

A form of housing often overlooked is the mobile home, once years ago regarded as a caravan and a rather inferior type of dwelling. For many people the image remains yet, despite the fact that the caravans of yesteryear have evolved into well-appointed units, linked to all the normal main services — water, gas, electricity, drains — and which bear comparison in every respect with two, three or four bedroom bungalows.

The two main criticisms are that:

- unlike a normal dwelling, the capital value shrinks steadily, and
- the materials used are not as durable as bricks and mortar. In consequence the 'life' of a unit is strictly limited.

Those in the mobile home industry say such strictures are a left-over from the days when a caravan was adapted to form a static home, that modern materials compare favourably with those used in conventional buildings, and that in recent years mobile homes have appreciated in value.

Anyone investigating should satisfy himself on a large number of points, including not only charges for services and the provision of amenities on the site itself, but also the availability of essential facilities in the surrounding districts.

Sheltered and not-so-sheltered housing

Sheltered housing is usually explained as grouped housing for elderly people who, while living their own independent life in their own self-contained units, may be vulnerable because of their age and require some degree of care supplied by a warden. The warden's job is to keep an unobtrusive and friendly eye on residents and to respond to an emergency signal for help.

A transformation has taken place in the sheltered housing schemes available. The main influence at work is the private construction industry. Builders have discovered that a new and expanding market for the supply of purpose-built dwellings for retired people, normally home owners, has come into existence.

In the past, home owners received a low priority in qualifying for this form of housing. Local authorities and housing associations, often in co-operation, supplied accommodation on a rental basis for council tenants and for those with insufficient capital to provide a roof of their own. Today, thanks to the builders, there are innumerable developments of grouped housing available to anyone, normally on a leasehold basis. All levels of the market are catered for. Schemes embrace luxury flats in country houses, village-type retirement communities and purpose-built blocks of flats. Grouped housing can also be made up of a mix of dwellings — flats, bungalows and, in some cases, three and even four bedroom houses. Basically, the emphasis is on accommodation providing one or two bedrooms.

Although the appeal is to the older-retired, there are increasing numbers of the younger-retired who are beginning to opt for this form of housing. To widen the appeal to the younger age-group, who may mentally classify such housing as fit for only the really old, the sales line is changing. Increasingly the message is that here is a trouble-free home, where one can get on with enjoying an active retirement, with the assurance that the accommodation is eminently suitable not only now but when one grows older.

The process has often led to the warden becoming the secretary, the administrator or just the housekeeper. Indeed, in some cases, she has vanished entirely and the alarm system is linked to a central outside panel, under constant monitoring. The very word 'shelter' is becoming taboo; there is a marked preference for 'retirement home' and the premises are presented as units sensibly equipped to meet the needs of retirement.

It should be mentioned, in passing, that some builders in planning new estates open to all age groups are offering dwellings specifically for retired people which, they say, give the opportunity of living in a 'mixed' community. Such accommodation does not come under the heading of 'sheltered'.

Anyone interested in grouped housing should be satisfied on a number of points. Is the property freely marketable — provided that the purchaser is of the requisite age? (The age of entry to retirement homes is usually from fifty-five or sixty upwards.) Does the leaseholder retain the right to sell the residence himself and what proceeds, if any, are deducted from the selling price? Is there an obligation to contribute towards a sinking fund for major repairs? The length of lease and the amount of ground rent should be clearly set out.

The service charge generally covers all outside repairs and maintenance, the upkeep of gardens, estate lighting, property insurance and maintenance of the alarm system, as well as the cost of warden service. Ask if there are any extra costs and check on arrangements for increasing the charge.

Entry phones on all communal entrances are regarded as essential. The kind of management also requires scrutiny. Builders often enter into an agreement with a housing associ- ation so that the latter becomes responsible for the administra- tion and running of a scheme. Such organisations have had a long experience of specialised housing for older people and the link is of mutual benefit.

Finally, it is as well to be sure that the scheme is in a desirable area, with easy access to amenities and services.

Sources of further information

For straightforward house hunting in a particular area, apart from the round of estate agents in the locality, a study of both the editorial and advertising columns of the local press over some weeks gives a useful picture of the district. Lists of local organisations, recreational facilities and much similar infor- mation should be available from the public library or the town hall. A Citizens' Advice Bureau is also helpful.

For more about mobile homes, the Department of the Environ- ment issues a free booklet entitled *Mobile Homes — A Guide For Residents and Site Owners*, which answers many queries. There is also a publication which specialises in this particular subject and which provides a useful reader service: *Mobile Homes and Holiday Caravan*, Link House, Dingwall Avenue, Croydon CR9 2TA.

As a follow up to the section on sheltered and not-so-sheltered housing a list of builders engaged in the retirement housing market is obtainable free from New Homes Marketing Board, 82 Cavendish Street, London W1M 8AD.

The Housing Information Department, Age Concern, 60 Pit- cairn Road, Mitcham, Surrey CR4 3LL issues a *Buyer's Guide To Sheltered Housing*. Age Concern also supply information on housing provided by local authorities and housing associ- ations.

Local housing information — housing association and private

sector projects as well as residential homes — is obtainable from the local authority. Lists of housing associations on a regional basis are available from the Housing Corporation, Maple House, 149 Tottenham Court Road, London W1P 0BN.

For people who become incapable of living an independent life, through physical or mental infirmity, homes are provided by local authorities, by voluntary associations, by some housing associations and charities and by owners of private accommodation.

Much depends on personal and financial circumstances, but the social service department of a local authority can give detailed information covering a particular area and Age Concern also can supply guidance.

An interesting and fairly recent development in this connection in both the commercial and charitable field has been the concept of 'total care' facilities. The Abbeyfield Society, for example, is making facilities available so that when a member of one of their homes is unable to remain independent he can be transferred to a 'care' or nursing home unit. A large private builder, McCarthy and Stone, Ltd, which specialises entirely in sheltered housing, is also offering facilities of an hotel character, where people can be provided with full or partial nursing and support services.

Part Two
Financial Aspects

7 Introduction

In a Government survey it was revealed that fewer than six people in every hundred receive the benefit of advice or counselling on the subject of retirement. This average may be slowly improving, but it remains a fact that far too few people prepare properly for this important event. A recurring theme of this book is the need to plan ahead, the further ahead the better.

Undoubtedly one of the main concerns amongst those approaching retirement is the question of money. Many people wonder if there will be enough income to make ends meet, let alone enjoy a higher standard of living than they experienced during their working lives. To a very large extent, these fears can be overcome by some careful planning. The earnings/pension gap can be significantly reduced by making additional savings in the years running up to retirement. The sooner the savings start, the greater the end benefit, so the earlier you plan the better off you will be. It would be foolish to claim that by regularly investing a small sum you will receive an embarrassment of riches. However it is realistic to believe that a significant improvement in your retirement income can be achieved if you are prepared to make some extra saving, or perhaps rearrange your existing investments onto a more tax efficient basis.

The term retirement planning sounds rather forbidding and as a result there is a tendency to ignore the subject altogether, or at least put off the matter until the last minute. In reality retirement planning often involves some simple homework on your personal finances so that the necessary steps can then be taken to deal with any anticipated problems.

This guide is designed to help not only those who are a

number of years away from retirement, but also those who find themselves faced with retirement in the near future. Here it will be more of a question of what to do with your pension and savings rather than how to build up extra income.

As you will come to realise, this is a far from straightforward subject. Pension schemes, both state run and private, are complicated creatures and a good deal of thought will be needed when dealing with the matter.

On top of that, you are likely to exchange part of your pension for a sizeable cash sum, and this will need to be prudently invested. One glance at the financial pages of a Sunday newspaper will highlight the bewildering number of investment opportunities that exist, all of them promising a handsome return. Which one is best for you? This will depend on many factors, not least of which is how you stand as far as the taxman is concerned. You will need to formulate a proper investment strategy to make most use of your hard earned capital.

Inevitably there will be those who retire with a great deal of money and those with very little. The fortunate ones with an abundance of wealth may wish to explore ways in which they can minimise the tax liabilities, both during their lifetime and on their death. This could mean moving abroad to a country where the tax climate is more congenial or it may simply mean arranging their affairs in such a way as to reduce the impact of UK taxation.

At the other end of the spectrum are those with too little income, and here it may be necessary to take advantage of any additional financial help that is available.

Whatever position you find yourself in, it will almost certainly be the case that proper planning will help to increase the financial security of your retirement years. This guide will help to point you in the right direction, but you may well need to seek professional advice on the best course of action for your individual circumstances. As with planning, the earlier you seek advice the better.

Good advice is worth its weight in gold; it will enable you to receive the most up-to-date information on pension, tax and financial matters, and to act accordingly to gain the maximum benefit.

Your financial affairs should ideally be reviewed regularly, say once a year, with the help of a professional. This will dramatically improve your chances of ending up at retirement financially well prepared for the years ahead. It will also reduce the worry that most people experience when it comes to making complicated investment decisions. A problem shared is a problem halved, especially when you have an expert on your side.

So don't let financial worries cloud your old age. Start planning early and money problems will in all probability never arise.

Drawing up a budget

One aspect of planning ahead is drawing up a budget. It is important to know where you stand. You may have had quite a lot of surplus income when you were working, now you need to budget more carefully — especially if you are retiring on a fixed income. On the other hand, don't be unnecessarily despondent: your before tax income may go down but your income after tax may not be so far short of the take home pay you enjoyed while working. If you manage your money carefully you may well be able to live as well — or even better — than before.

The best approach is to make a list of your expenditure by taking a year's supply of your bank statements, cheque book stubs and statements from any credit card companies (ensure as far as possible that you have identified *all* your expenditure, noting any extraordinary items that do not occur on a regular basis). When this has been done, fill in the following table, making an allowance for any increase or decrease you expect to occur when you retire.

See over for table

Expenditure	Current year	Projected in retirement
House		
Rent or mortgage repayments		
General and water rates		
Repairs, maintenance and decoration		
Heating and lighting		
Telephone		
Household insurance		
Food and clothes		
Food and drink		
Pet food		
Clothes		
Transport and travel		
Car maintenance, petrol and oil		
Car tax, insurance and subs. to AA/RAC etc		
Other travel		
Recreation		
TV licence, TV and video rental		
Subscription		
Holidays		
Newspapers, periodicals and books		
Personal items		
Cigarettes, tobacco and beverages		
Hairdressing		
Gifts or deeds of covenant		
Spending money		
Regular saving and life assurance		
Any other major expenditure	———	———
Total	———	———

The table can be used by those who are planning some way ahead, as well as those who are about to stop working. Of course certain allowances must be made, especially by people who fall into the former category, but nevertheless it will be a useful exercise to compare your anticipated expenditure with what you expect to receive.

Asking yourself the right questions

This book is aimed at three different types of person:

(1)   A person planning ahead for retirement in the future;
(2)   Someone about to retire in the immediate future who wishes to maximise post retirement income;
(3)   A retired person who wants to know how he or she can pass on money and property to the family.

Let us look at the questions which should occupy each person's mind:

1 The person planning ahead

● Why are pension contributions the most tax efficient form of saving?
● What types of pension scheme are available?
● What can you do to improve the pension that you will receive from a former employer?
● Can you fund a pension for your wife?
● What is the best way to save your surplus income?

2 The person about to retire

● What State benefits are available?
● How can you make the most of your entitlement under company pension schemes?
● Should you take a tax free lump sum in lieu of part of your pension?
● What tax will you pay after retirement?
● How can you save tax?
● What happens if you carry on working on a part-time basis?
● How can you make the most of your savings?
● What types of investment are available, how do they work, what are their pros and cons?
● How do you go about setting up a portfolio and managing your investments?
● What can you do if you have to retire on a low income?
● What are the things to consider if you want to retire abroad?
● What do you need to bear in mind if you are coming back to the UK from abroad or are a foreigner who is retiring in the UK?

3 The person who is concerned about how to pass on his or her money

● What will happen if you don't make a Will?
● How should you go about making one, who should you appoint as executors etc?
● How is inheritance tax charged?
● What steps can you take to reduce the burden of this tax?

Most elderly people are reluctant to take action which will significantly reduce their spendable income or curtail their financial independence or flexibility. This is understandable. On the other hand, people in this position want to know about inheritance tax to see whether there is relatively simple action which they could take which would help them to reduce the burden of the inheritance tax which will eventually fall upon their family. If ways can be put forward of saving inheritance tax without giving up substantial income or losing flexibility, these are often favourably received.

The above questions are addressed in that order in the text and whilst we hope that you will read the book right through we have given you the page references so that you can 'dip in' to those sections which particularly interest you.

Some of the terminology is quite technical. We have tried to keep things simple and avoid jargon but you may find the glossary at the end of this book to be helpful. Finally, we set out in the appendix a list of free Government Publications which you may find useful.

8 Funding your retirement

This chapter is aimed at someone who is middle-aged and planning for his or her retirement — although some of the information is of more general relevance.

We seek to deal with the following questions:

- Why is advance planning so vital?
- Why are pension contributions the most tax efficient form of saving?
- What types of pension scheme are available?
- What can you do to improve the pension that you will receive from a former employer?
- Can you fund a pension for your wife?
- What is the best way to save out of surplus income?
- What can be done at the last minute?

Why is advance planning so vital?

It can't be emphasised too strongly that life divides into two parts, your working life when you earn a salary, and the period after your retirement when you live off the income generated by your savings. Once you have stopped earning there will be nothing that you can do to supplement your savings, although you can of course change the way in which they are invested so as to produce additional income.

Your savings include your pension scheme and also the contributions that you have paid into the state pension scheme (these are, in effect, 'compulsory' savings). Pension schemes are the most efficient way of saving — because of the tax benefits — and hence we focus particularly on this aspect of funding your retirement income. However, there are also ways of building up your capital to supplement your post retirement income and it is important to consider these if you want to take full advantage of the opportunities that retirement provides.

You have probably given your early working years to your family, spending most of your income on housing and food (and possibly the education of your children), now is the time to think of yourself and your spouse. Sound planning will enable you to make use of the extra free time that you will have and to do things such as travel, voluntary work, hobbies etc — all the things that the commitments of a career have prevented you from doing. If you don't plan ahead your retirement may be clouded by financial problems.

The state benefits (see p 106) may be sufficient to keep the wolf from the door but even with the additional pension under the State Earnings Related Pension Scheme they are unlikely to allow you to continue your present life style, let alone expand your expenditure on those extras which make life enjoyable. If you are self-employed the state benefits are even less satisfactory because SERPS does not apply to you at all.

The sooner you start, the better. If you and/or your employer fund your pension by making contributions at the rate of say 10 per cent of your earnings, the pension will be dramatically better if you start to do this well before retirement. The following table illustrates this:

Age when contributions start	Pensions as a proportion of your final earnings	
	Retirement at age 60	Retirement at age 65
Male aged 35	35.8	48.9
Female aged 35	33.0	44.5
Male aged 40	27.3	38.7
Female aged 40	25.2	35.2
Male aged 45	19.5	29.4
Female aged 45	18.1	26.8
Male aged 50	12.5	21.1
Female aged 50	11.5	19.2
Male aged 55	5.9	13.5
Female aged 55	5.4	12.3

Assumptions

These figures assume that the retirement fund built up by your contributions grows at 12 per cent and that your earnings increase by an average of 10 per cent per annum. The pensions are based on current annuity rates as at December 1986.

It is also possible to have a pension that increases by up to 8 per cent each year to help to protect your income against inflation. If you choose this option, your *starting* pension will be about 50 per cent of the figures shown in the table.

The figures shown are for single lives — however, if you want a pension that will continue during the lifetime of yourself *and* your spouse, then you will have to settle for a lower amount.

Why are pension schemes the most tax efficient form of saving?

Most people are aware that pension plans offer one of the best means of saving for retirement. At present pension plans have three distinct advantages over other forms of long-term savings:

(*a*)   pension funds are exempt from all UK taxes, and accordingly the fund accumulates at a higher rate than other forms of savings;
(*b*)   at retirement part of the pension may be commuted for a tax-free lump sum;
(*c*)   up to certain limits, pension contributions attract tax relief up to the highest rate of tax.

Many self-employed people take the view that 'their business is their pension scheme'. However, this can often be short-sighted as the profitability of the business may decline if you try to continue in business when you should have retired. Furthermore, even if you are still as efficient at age 70 as you were when you were building up the business, the fact remains that if something happens to you, the value of the business will be affected. How will your widow stand then?

Another way in which this kind of thinking is faulty is that it ignores the considerable tax benefits and reliefs enjoyed by pension funds. After tax, £1,000 of profits may be reduced to as little as £400 and it is only this depleted sum which works for you. In contrast £1,000 put into a pension contribution is worth £1,000 of savings, and the return earned on that £1,000 is tax free. If we assume that the £1,000 earns a return of 12 per cent the fund will be worth £3,105 in ten years time. *After tax income of £400 (ie £1,000 less 60 per cent tax) has to grow at the rate of nearly 23 per cent per annum to build up a similar amount over the same period.*

What types of pension scheme are available?

Company pension schemes

Company or 'private' pension schemes operated by your employer are also sometimes called 'occupational' pension schemes. The benefits under such schemes can vary considerably: one problem is that for many years the emphasis in the legislation was on making sure that the benefits provided were not too generous. Legislation requiring *minimum* benefits is a relatively recent thing whereas all schemes have to comply with limits laid down by the Inland Revenue.

The maximum pension permitted by the Inland Revenue is two thirds of your 'final remuneration' ie salary and most other taxable earnings at the date of retirement. This can be provided to anyone who has achieved ten years service but in practice it is very rare for a company scheme to be as generous as this.

In practice most schemes provide a pension of one sixtieth of final salary for each year of service. This provides the maximum pension of two thirds final salary only for a person who has worked with the company for 40 years. It is, however, increasingly common for additional benefits to be given to senior staff who have joined late in their career.

The definition of final salary is often complex in order to protect a person whose earnings suffer a fall in the last year or two of his working life. If you are concerned to compare the details of the scheme to which you belong with others, there is the excellent *Allied Dunbar Pensions Guide* which covers the subject. Bear in mind, however, that the 1987 Budget outlined new rules which apply to people who join a pension scheme on or after 17 March 1987. If you fall into this category you may find that you can receive the maximum two-thirds pension only if you achieve 20 years' service. There could also be restrictions on the maximum tax-free lump sum that you can take.

The most important thing to do is to establish exactly what benefits you will get under your company scheme and this can best be done by consulting your employer. So as a first step you should compare your expected pension to the maximum that the Inland Revenue will permit you to have. If there is any shortfall, then think about ways to top it up.

Topping up a company pension scheme

As we have said, it is in fact quite rare for a person to be entitled to as much from a pension scheme as the Inland Revenue would allow him to have; if you are in this position, you should take every opportunity to improve your pension. Why not make use of a scheme which permits you to pay money as additional voluntary contributions to improve your pension? Many employers have these additional voluntary contributions (AVC) schemes, and this should be your first line of enquiry. If your employer does not operate an AVC scheme then from October 1987 you can take advantage of one run by an independent financial institution such as an insurance company or building society.

Everyone is free to contribute up to 15 per cent of their income towards a pension scheme and claim full tax relief. In practice, few pension schemes require obligatory contributions on anything like this scale. So the difference between the 5 per cent or 6 per cent which you may be obliged to contribute to the main pension scheme and the full 15 per cent entitlement can be paid in AVCs. Not only is full tax relief available on these contributions, but the funds accumulate free of UK tax until retirement. At that time they are treated in exactly the same way as any other pension entitlement, except that AVC plans started after 7 April do not produce a tax free lump sum.

An AVC could be used when someone anticipates that he will not otherwise be able to afford to commute part of his pension from the main scheme for cash. Under an AVC scheme a person obtains relief at source at the maximum rate of tax which applies to his earnings — usually a minimum of 27 per cent. In addition, the growth within the fund is free from income tax and CGT which will obviously produce a much better result than a comparable investment that is subject to tax.

Salary sacrifice

A salary sacrifice arrangement is one where an individual gives up some of his salary, with the amount that has been given up being paid by his or her employer into an approved pension scheme. Income tax relief is obtained at the individual's top rate because the amount given up no longer forms part of his taxable income. It is also possible to sacrifice bonus payments to achieve the same result. Salary sacrifice arrangements are especially attractive for the high income earner. There can also be a useful saving in the employer's national insurance contributions because the company saves 10.45 per cent of the amount given up by the employee. This saving may enable the employer to increase its contributions and thus pass on the benefit of the saving to the employee.

A salary sacrifice requires the agreement of both the company and the employee and must be properly documented in order to obtain Inland Revenue approval. Provided the right procedures are followed, the advantages are considerable, especially for those who would not otherwise receive an adequate company pension.

Personal pension schemes

If you do not belong to a company pension scheme or if you are self-employed then you may arrange a personal pension scheme. Like a company scheme member, the amount you may contribute is laid down by the Inland Revenue and at the present time the limits are as follows:

Born in 1934 onwards	$17\frac{1}{2}$%
1916 to 1933	20%
1914 to 1915	21%
1912 to 1913	24%

New personal pension plans from 4 January 1988

Age	
up to 50	$17\frac{1}{2}$%
51–55	20%
56–60	$22\frac{1}{2}$%
61–75	$27\frac{1}{2}$%

These percentages apply to 'net relevant earnings' which can be broadly defined as earnings from your non-pensionable employment or business, less certain deductions such as expenses, trading losses, capital allowances etc.

If you are in the position of having two sources of income, one from pensionable employment and the other being net relevant earnings, you may contribute up to the above limit in respect of your net relevant earnings regardless of the level of your pensionable earnings. So you can have two pensions, one provided by your employer and the other provided by you out of your own pocket.

In addition to the above limits, you are also allowed to make a contribution in respect of unpaid contributions during the previous six years. Thus for those making their first retirement contributions in the 1987/88 tax year, an additional sum may also be paid in respect of 1981/82 and subsequent years. As a means of providing for retirement this is an especially useful allowance.

If you wish to gain the maximum benefit from your pension contributions then the sooner they are paid the better. The following table which is based upon typical assumptions on investment return (12 per cent per annum) illustrates this point vividly.

Annual pension contribution £1,000.00 (£730 net relief at 27%)	
Age next birthday (Man)	*Estimated pension fund at age 60*
	£
35	148,000
40	80,000
45	42,000
50	20,000

As the figures show, a delay of five years in starting a pension is expensive and may also cause a considerable burden in later years as an effort is made to make up for the lost time. Any insurance company, actuary or other qualified advisor will strongly recommend that you start a pension plan as soon as you can afford to do so.

Self-employed pensions

Self-employed people pay a lower rate of national insurance contributions than the combined employers/employees contributions. This is one of the few fiscal benefits enjoyed by self-employed people. If you simply put the difference, or 'saving', into a private pension plan you could build up significant benefits.

Example

A makes profits of £30,000. If he carried on the business through a company and took out a salary of £30,000 the following amounts would be payable as National Insurance Contributions:

Payable by A personally	£1,333
Payable by company	3,135
	4,468

As A is self-employed the maximum payable for 1986/87 is £848 (Class II £195, Class IV £653).

Thus A could afford to put away private pension contributions of £3,620 and still be no worse off than if he had carried on his business through a company. Paying contributions at this rate from age 40 would produce a substantial pension—according to our assumptions the pension available at age 65 would represent about 20% of his final earnings.

As before this projection is based on a rate of growth of 12 per cent and on the basis that earnings will grow at 10 per cent per annum. The annuity rate chosen is that available at December 1986.

What can you do to improve the pension that you will receive from a former employer?

It is well known that people who have changed jobs ('early leavers') have lost out in terms of pension. As a general practice, the most that an early leaver used to be able to expect was a frozen pension and this could lead to very unfair results.

Example

A has done 40 years service with one company. He retires on a final salary of £24,000. He might well receive a pension of 40/60 × 24,000, ie £16,000.

B worked for 20 years with one company and his salary on leaving amounted to £5,000. He then worked for the same company as A and retired on a salary of £30,000. B's pension income is likely to be made up of two parts:

pension from first employer	
20/60 × salary on leaving of £5,000	1,667
pension from second employer	
20/60 × final salary of £30,000	10,000
	11,667

Whereas A gets a pension of nearly 67% of his final earnings, B gets pensions which amount to only 39% of his final salary.

Recent legislation has improved the position for the early leaver, but you should still carefully explore your pension position if you decide to change jobs or if you have changed jobs in the past.

Transfer values

One way to reduce this problem is to arrange for a transfer value to be paid from the trustees of your former employer's pension scheme into your new pension scheme. However, the terms have to be negotiated between the actuaries involved and you may find that a transfer value which reflects the value of your future benefits in respect of (say) ten years past service buys the equivalent of only (say) six years benefits under your new scheme. This is very much an area where you need professional advice.

Buy-out bonds

Another option which is now available as of right in respect of post 1985 service is to arrange for the trustees of your former employer's pension scheme to purchase a deferred annuity contract under the provisions of FA 1981, s 32. These 'buy out' or 'section 32' bonds may offer better value than a transfer value — but once again you should obtain professional advice on the implications in your particular situation.

Future legislation

'Portable' pensions are what the public want and the Government has committed itself to passing legislation to remove barriers to this. Most of the legislation is expected to come into force by January 1988, but these reforms have probably come too late for those who are in a company pension scheme and are already into the last third of their working life.

Those who are self-employed may be affected if they wish to enter into a new pension policy after January 1988. From this date there will be a new variety of pension plans, but these will not be significantly different from their predecessors.

Can you fund a pension for your wife?

Many business and professional people employ their wives, mainly on a part-time basis where the salary is insufficient to attract income tax and National Insurance contributions. Where this happens, and provided the main income is taxed under Schedule D, it is possible to arrange a pension scheme for the wife who is technically an employee. There are four significant advantages in doing so; the first three may be obvious but the fourth is not.

Firstly, the contributions paid into the pension scheme are treated as a business expense and thus qualify for tax relief. Secondly, there is the attraction of investing money in a tax exempt fund. Thirdly, a pension scheme may be an effective 'tax shelter' for those who pay tax at the higher rates because the pension shelters the growth on the contributions and repays them with the interest when your tax liabilities are lower. Fourthly, when the pension is paid to the wife it qualifies for treatment as earned income in her hands. This means that the wife's earned income allowance is offset against the pension and thus a significant amount of the income will not suffer tax. Also remember that there will be the right to take out a tax free cash sum.

It may well be that the salary involved is low and you may think that such an arrangement would not be worthwhile. This is certainly not so. As we explained in a previous chapter, the maximum pension that an employee can receive at retirement is two thirds of his salary at that time. In order to ensure that people are not unduly restricted in terms of their pension contributions, the Inland Revenue will allow the employee's present-day salary to be increased by 8.5 per cent per year to their normal retirement date, and approve contributions that will fund a pension of two thirds of that sum. Thus it is possible for worthwhile amounts to be paid even though the current salary appears not to justify them. In many cases putting money into a pension scheme on behalf of your spouse is more tax efficient than paying contributions for yourself.

Example

Husband age 50 employs his wife age 48 on a salary of £1,800 a year. She will have achieved 20 years' service by age 60.

The current salary of £1,800 is assumed to increase at 8.5% a year to age 60, making a final pensionable salary of approximately £4,700.

Pension can be provided to 2/3rds of £4,700 (say)	£3,100
Pension premium of £90.00 per month paid by husband produces a pension fund at age 60 (assuming growth at 12%)	£23,400
After tax relief at 27% the husband pays out total contributions of	£9,460.80
Wife receives—tax free cash sum	
(1.5 times final salary)	£7,050.00
plus lifetime pension (based on a pension rate of 10%)	£1,635.00

As the pension is less than the wife's earned income relief then there is no income tax to pay on the pension. So you get the unbeatable combination of tax relief on your savings, investment in a tax free fund, a tax free lump sum at retirement plus an income on which you do not have to pay tax.

What is the best way to save out of surplus income?

Having done all you can to maximise your pension, a further way of supplementing your retirement income is to save regularly from after-tax income in order to produce a lump sum at age 60 or 65. There are numerous schemes for just this purpose but some are not particularly tax efficient — especially if you are subject to the higher rates of income tax.

If you are a higher rate tax payer you need a scheme that will shelter the return on your savings from the ravages of tax and there is a sound argument for an endowment policy issued by an insurance company (often known as a 'maximum investment plan'). The income and capital growth earned by the insurance company on the money that you put into an endowment policy is taxed at life assurance company rates (29 per cent–35 per cent) rather than at the rates which apply to your personal income. Thus a saving scheme of this type is still treated in a favourable way for tax purposes and continues to have attractions despite the abolition of life assurance premium relief in 1984. After a certain period, normally seven and a half years, you can cash in your policy and the amounts that you will then receive are totally free of tax.

There are other regular saving schemes which offer attractive returns for relatively small sums of money. Look at the National Savings yearly plan which guarantees a competitive rate of return especially to those who are liable to higher rates of tax. Up to £200 per month can be salted away under this arrangement and the return is totally tax free. Alternatively, a unit trust savings plan could be most useful. This ensures a gradual build up of units and it is possible under most plans for your contributions to be spread between several different unit trusts.

The Government recently introduced a further type of scheme, the personal equity plan (PEP). This enables you to build up a portfolio of ordinary shares and unit trusts by saving a regular sum. You can put in up to £200 per month, £2,400 per year, and your spouse can make a similar contribution.

Personal equity plans enjoy two types of tax relief. Firstly, the income within the plan is exempt from income tax. Secondly, there is no capital gains tax on disposals of investments by the PEP managers. These tax incentives may seem relatively modest, but if you were to put the maximum amount into a personal equity plan for five or six, or even ten years, the total amount invested within the plan could be very substantial and the tax benefits would then also be very substantial.

You can cash the plan in at any stage but the tax benefits will be clawed back if you cash in too quickly — the minimum period that you must keep your personal equity plan going in order to avoid forfeiting your tax reliefs depends upon when you start the plan. The minimum period could be as short as one year and a day and could be as long as two years.

Regardless of which particular type of regular savings plan you use, the most important thing is to start as soon as possible. Even modest amounts saved regularly over a ten year period can produce worthwhile results. So start now at a level that you can comfortably afford and increase this as and when possible.

The earlier you start the more you will accumulate. Watch the sums grow as the wonder of compound growth takes effect!

Example

A person saves £250.00 a year.

Number of years payments	Total sum saved	Value of savings with interest at		
		6%	8%	10%
5	£1250	£1493	£1583	£1679
10	£2500	£3493	£3911	£4382
15	£3750	£6168	£7331	£8737

Tax efficient capital investments

Whereas some people will wish to create a capital sum for retirement, others may have capital already which they wish to invest on a medium/long-term basis in a tax efficient way. In these cases, investment bonds issued by insurance companies may be attractive as the growth in the bond is not liable to income tax until such time as the investment is cashed in, and then is liable only to tax at the higher rates. This means in effect that you can use an investment bond to defer a tax charge.

Example

(1) £10,000 invested in bonds for 10 years at 8% growth will be worth £21,589. Assuming tax is paid at 60% the liability is 33% on the gain of £11,589 (ie £3,824) and the net proceeds are then £17,765.

(2) £10,000 invested in a building society for 10 years at 8% net at the basic rate of tax. Assuming 60% tax is paid throughout the investment term the equivalent net return is approximately 4.5%. Thus the net value of the investment after 10 years is £15,530. These values are approximate as the higher rate tax liability is not deducted at source and, therefore, it is difficult to calculate the exact compound rate.

Very often people can effectively shelter investment income until after retirement at which time they may be subject to a much lower rate of tax.

The above example assumes that the year in which the bond is redeemed is one in which tax is paid at 60 per cent. The bond could however be cashed in a year when tax is payable at a much lower rate. Alternatively the bond could be 'gifted' to children or grandchildren in which case they could then cash the bond without a tax liability and thus retain the whole £21,589. This assumes that the recipient is a basic rate taxpayer.

Another way of deferring your taxable income and thus reducing your tax bill is to invest in an offshore 'roll-up' fund. Roll-up funds are operated by leading UK financial institutions using companies based offshore in the Isle of Man or Channel Islands. The funds themselves invest in bank deposits and very short term fixed interest investments. The income from these investments is not distributed as dividends but added to the share price, or 'rolled-up'. The funds operate in a similar way to unit trusts so that the investor realises the benefits of the accumulated income when he sells his shares. The profit is subject to income tax, but the investor can choose the year in which he has the taxable income. Very often a person can achieve an advantage by investing in a roll-up fund during his high earning years when interest would normally have attracted a higher rate of tax and then selling the shares in a year in which his taxable income is much lower. Another aspect is that whilst the capital remains invested in the roll-up fund, the money is accumulating interest often without any tax whatsoever!

There are many other lump sum investment schemes which also enjoy favourable tax treatment. National Savings Certificates are a good example. You may well find it worthwhile to shop around and spread your capital across a number of different investments which enjoy tax advantages.

Of course, quite apart from the taxation aspects, it can make sense to spread your investments. Tax is only one aspect and there are other considerations such as the fact that you may need access to some of your capital in an emergency, you may want to invest some in an all-out pursuit of capital growth etc. Our section on fixed interest and capital growth investments is aimed mainly at people who have already retired and who are investing their capital but much of the detailed analysis of the way in which different types of investments work will also be of interest if you are looking ten years ahead.

What can be done at the last minute?

When a person draws near to his retirement date it is worth considering whether additional voluntary contributions or personal pension contributions can be paid. Even though the money may be with the insurance company for a relatively short time, the fact that the contributions attract income tax relief and a lump sum may be taken tax-free means that there is often substantial advantage in paying such contributions. Here are two typical examples to illustrate the possible benefits:

Example

A woman approaching 60 decided to pay a personal pension contribution. A single payment of £1,000 would attract 27% income tax relief and so the net cost would be only £730. If she took the benefits 6 months later she might expect to receive a tax-free lump sum of £300 plus an on-going pension of £92 per annum.

The benefits can be even greater for a person who is subject to tax at the maximum rate of 60 per cent.

Example

A man aged 64 is due to retire on his 65th birthday in three months' time. If he pays £5,000 personal pension premiums the following position is likely to obtain:

Retirement Annuity Premium	£5,000
less tax relief at 60%	£3,000
	£2,000
less tax free lump sum	£1,370
Net cost	£ 630

In return for this net outlay, he could expect to receive an on-going pension of £380 per annum.

The amount which may be taken as a tax free lump sum may be slightly less for pension policies effected after 31 December 1987, but the on-going pension will be correspondingly increased.

Don't forget that you can pay personal pension premiums if you have non-pensionable earnings even though you may also have pensionable earnings from another employment.

9 Planning your pension

Most people when they retire become entitled to a number of different pensions. To begin with there is the state basic retirement pension, in addition to which there may well be benefits from the state earnings related scheme. On top of these, it is likely in many cases that the individual will also be entitled to a pension from his employer's pension scheme, or from a personal pension plan in the case of those who were either in non-pensionable employment or who were self-employed.

This chapter sets out the position regarding your pension benefits and describes some of the alternatives that you may encounter. We also explain two options which may be open to you.

● Should you commute, ie give up part of your pension in return for a tax free lump sum?
● Can you transfer your private pension fund to another insurance company that offers better annuity rates?

State pensions

The starting point for anyone concerned about their income in retirement must be to establish exactly what pension can be expected from the state. There is some confusion in the minds of many people about this subject because of all the changes that have taken place in the past. In 1978 a completely new pension scheme was introduced which has yet to take full effect. However, for those people retiring today there is often a useful pension from this source.

At present the state retirement pension can be divided into two parts.

Basic retirement pension

The basic retirement pension is applicable to everybody whether employed or self-employed. At the time of writing, this is currently £38.70 per week for a single person and £61.95 per week for a married couple. This is raised by the Government in line with the Retail Price Index in April of each year.

To qualify for the full amount you must be 65 (for a man) or 60 (for a woman) and have paid sufficient National Insurance contributions during your working life; this is defined as paying contributions for about 90 per cent of your working life between the ages of 16 and 65 (or 60 for women). For those who have not satisfied these conditions, a reduced pension will be paid. You should receive a pension claim form from the Department of Health and Social Security about four months before you retire and if you do not receive this, then you should make enquiries at your local DHSS office.

If you are a married woman and your husband is still working, a pension can still be claimed at the rate applicable to the single person provided you are aged 60 and you have paid enough National Insurance contributions in your own right. If you satisfy the contribution conditions only in part, you may get a lower rate. When your husband retires you can then claim the full married woman's rate (£23.25) if this is higher.

Where a married woman has not paid sufficient contributions to earn her own pension then she must wait until her husband retires. Then she can claim a pension based on her husband's contributions. A degree of care must be exercised in this regard, as there are a number of alternatives available and the choice of pension will depend on individual circumstances.

Graduated pension

Before the state earnings related pension scheme was introduced, there was another scheme in force known as the state graduated pension scheme. You may be entitled to some benefits from this in addition to the state earnings related pension, but the extra amount is not significant.

State earnings related scheme

The state earnings related scheme was introduced in 1978. The full name of the scheme is the state earnings related pension scheme, hence the term 'SERPS'. It is intended to improve the position of employees who are not in a company pension scheme and to provide an earnings related pension which will be payable in addition to the basic state pension.

The state earnings related scheme will take full effect in 1998 after it has been going for twenty years and will provide a pension related to earnings between two bands (known as the upper and lower earnings limits). The amount that you get will therefore depend upon your earnings but, because the upper earnings limit is relatively low, the maximum pension from this source is unlikely to be sufficient for a comfortable retirement. For example, if the scheme had been going for twenty years the maximum pension which would now be payable would be approximately £3,200 per annum.

On the other hand, the SERPS scheme is index-linked so that the pension is increased each year in line with inflation and this can make it a most valuable benefit even given the fact that no-one who retires at present is entitled to the full pension which will only be available once the scheme has been running for twenty years.

In 1987/88 the lower earnings limit is £169.00 per month and the upper limit is £1,278.33. Each year's earnings are revalued annually until normal retirement in line with movements in national average earnings. In consequence, a person retiring in April 1987 whose earnings have exceeded the upper earnings limit throughout the scheme will be entitled to receive an additional pension of approximately £28 per week. Thereafter the pension, like the basic retirement pension, is linked to the retail price index.

At present a widow may inherit the whole of her husband's earnings related pension but this entitlement will eventually be reduced to 50 per cent. This change will, however, not take place until the year 2000.

The scheme does not affect everyone. In order to benefit from SERPS you must be 'contracted in' which means that you and your employer pay higher National Insurance contributions. If you work for an employer then you will be in SERPS unless you have been 'contracted out' — in which case there is no need to worry because this will mean that you are a member of a company pension scheme that is at least as good as SERPS. It is possible, however, to be a member of SERPS *and* a member of a company pension scheme and this is particularly beneficial where you have earnings in excess of the 'upper earnings limit'. It will also mean that you can fund for the maximum pension of 2/3 salary in addition to your SERPS pension.

State pensions are useful, especially since they are linked to the cost of living or earnings and will retain their value. The basic retirement pension makes a significant contribution to either a single person's or a married couple's budget and the state earnings related pension already provides a useful addition to this. In a few more years it will be much more important.

Self-employed persons

Those who are self-employed cannot be eligible for SERPS and therefore will qualify only for the basic state retirement pension.

Private pensions

About half the people who work for companies belong to occupational pension schemes as well as the state ones. Some of these are contracted out of SERPS, whereas others operate on top of it. If you are contracted out you will not receive an earnings related pension from the state but your private pension must be at least equal to the state pension and will almost certainly produce better benefits. In most cases, a private scheme will provide a pension which is vastly better than that available from the state and no doubt there will be a number of options to choose from at retirement.

Choosing a pension

When members of pension schemes retire they are usually given a choice of how they wish the income to be paid. It is possible to have a pension which will only continue for as long as one person survives. Alternatively, they can choose a smaller pension which will continue throughout the life of both husband and wife (known as joint life pension). The size of the reduction depends upon their ages. If they are both 65, a fund of £10,000 could provide them with a lifetime income of, for example, £1,275 per year. For the same fund a single man of 65 could expect £1,550 a year.

The exact pension would, of course, depend on rates available in the market at retirement.

The choice of the appropriate type of pension depends upon individual circumstances. A popular choice for married couples is a joint life pension which reduces to a lower amount after the first death. This protects the survivor but recognises the fact that one can live more cheaply than two.

Commuting your company pension for cash

It is normal for a person at retirement to be given the option of exchanging part of the pension for a tax-free lump sum. This is a valuable benefit but many people are not sure whether it is really to their advantage to cash in their pension and have difficulty making up their minds whether or not to take advantage of the opportunity.

At first sight, the choice between a tax-free sum now and taxable pension seems straightforward. Even if you do not need the lump sum now, it seems more sensible to take it. This may, however, be an oversimplification and some people may be better off with the pension.

The Inland Revenue restricts the size of the tax-free lump sum which can be given. The maximum allowed is one and a half times a person's final remuneration (including benefits in kind), but smaller amounts must be given to those with less than 20 years' service. The most critical question is how much pension must be sacrificed in return for the lump sum. There is a table of factors which has been agreed among the insurance companies and the actuaries who run independent pension schemes:

	Age	Factor
Men	60	10.2
	65	9.0
	70	7.8
Women	55	12.2
	60	11.0
	65	9.8

The factors for other ages can be calculated by an increase or decrease of 0.02 per month of age. In order to calculate the reduction in pension, the lump sum should be divided by it. Thus, a woman retiring at 60 and receiving a tax-free lump sum of £11,000 would have her pension reduced by £1,000 per annum. A pension scheme does not have to use these factors and can choose others which are more or less favourable.

Is commuting pensions worthwhile?

Example

A man of 65 commutes £2,000 worth of pension (£1,460 after tax of 27%) for a cash sum of £18,000. He can invest this money in a purchased life annuity from a life company. This will give him a gross income of £2,800 at December 1986 rates. £1,260 of it will be tax-free, (known as the capital content) leaving only £1,540 taxable. This gives a net income after basic rate tax of £2,284 in contrast to £1,460 from the pension. By taking the cash sum and reinvesting it, the net income after tax has increased by £924.

Pensions and inflation

Our example is a perfectly valid comparison if the pension from the company scheme is properly comparable to the annuity which has been bought from the insurance company (see *Annuities* on p 229). However, the two will not always be comparable because a great many superannuation schemes will increase pensions in course of payment. Insurance companies do not do this for annuities unless it is part of the contract.

This factor can make it difficult to compare the benefit of giving up pension for a cash sum. If inflation revives and the pension scheme increases the benefit in payment to match it, the income payable will soon overtake any annuity which can be purchased for the cash sum. On the other hand, inflation may continue to decline and even if it does not, the pension scheme may not keep pace with it.

Pensions in the public sector normally match inflation, but few private ones do this. However, a high proportion of the major employers in the private sector make discretionary increase to pensions in payment and in recent years these have tended to match inflation.

There are a few private pension schemes in which the pension increases automatically after retirement. When this is the case, the commutation value of the pension will be different. In effect you will get more cash for each pound of pension surrendered.

The best way of assessing your own position is to find out the record of your employer over the last few years. If there is no contractual obligation on the company to continue making increases, there is a strong moral one. If pensions have kept pace with the cost of living in the past then it is likely that they will do so in the future. If they have not done so, then you should not expect them to in the future unless you have clear evidence of a change of heart. In the absence of any increase it is clearly to your advantage to take the cash sum. If, on the other hand, you can expect a pension which will more or less keep pace with inflation the decision is much more finely balanced. On pure investment grounds you are probably better off to stick with the highest possible pension, although this could be a mistake if inflation continues to reduce.

Of course, investment considerations are not the only ones. If the pension you will receive is more than sufficient after commuting a portion and you have uses for the cash you should of course take it. The fact remains that many people find that as retirement approaches they have more than sufficient cash and when this is the case they can simply choose the most financially advantageous arrangement.

Personal pension plans

Where you have paid personal pension premiums, ie you have contributed to a personal pension scheme unconnected to an employer, then commutation is a reasonably straightforward matter. Current legislation allows the insurance company to pay a tax-free lump sum which of course requires the surrender of part of the pension entitlement. However, in most cases it is advantageous to take the cash and reinvest in a purchased life annuity, with its tax-free 'capital content' as described above. This feature, therefore, restricts the tax charge to only the interest element of the annuity and accordingly the after tax income is higher than it would be from the pension which is wholly taxable.

Open market options

Certain types of pension scheme offer what is known as an open market option. This enables a person to 'shop around' at the time of his retirement and use the funds which he has accumulated with one insurance company to buy an annuity from another if their rates are better. In practice, there is a considerable difference in annuity rates and it is well worth looking around to ensure that the annuity quoted to you by your own insurance company is the best rate available.

As an indication of the amount of variation, the rates quoted by two insurance companies in December 1986 for a single life annuity for a man aged 65 and a fund of £10,000 varied from £1,477 to £1,530 per annum.

It should be noted that some insurance companies impose a 'transfer fee' or charge where a fund is transferred to another insurance company. Other companies give a 'loyalty bonus', ie the normal annuity rates are enhanced for people who have had a pension contract with the company concerned. Even so, it is still well worth obtaining competitive quotations (if an open market option forms part of your pension arrangements).

Widow's pension

When deciding on the type of pension that most suits your requirements, bear in mind that under the state scheme the widow's pension is limited to the amount payable to a single person (provided she is widowed after age 60). This boils down to the basic retirement pension for a single person plus the amount payable under the earnings related scheme. Therefore it may well be advisable to choose a pension that continues during the lifetime of your widow.

Invalidity benefit

If you are drawing invalidity benefit then when you reach age 65 (if you are a man) or 60 (if you are female) you must decide whether you wish to continue to do so for a further five years, or elect to take the basic retirement pension instead. In some cases this may not be a straightforward matter because these two benefits are not treated in the same way by the Inland Revenue.

Since November 1980, invalidity benefit has not been subject to income tax whereas state pensions are fully taxable. So this presents a problem and the choice will depend on the amount of income you will enjoy apart from either the invalidity benefit or state pension. To resolve the matter, add up all your other gross income (that is the amount before tax is taken off) such as private pensions, building society interest, etc. If the total of these items is greater than your personal allowance then you should retain the invalidity benefit. This will save you paying the extra tax that would arise if you decide to draw the basic retirement pension.

10 Tax does matter

It would be foolish to try to ignore the effect of taxation. We all wish income tax had 'never happened' but the only sensible course of action is to calculate what is involved (ie 'compute' your tax liability) and then take whatever steps are available to reduce its impact. This chapter begins by setting out the way in which you can work out your income tax bill and describes the way in which capital gains tax operates. As part of this we deal with three matters:

● How is age allowance computed?
● How top-slicing relief applies when you dispose of an investment bond
● How does the CGT main residence exemption work?

We then address the following questions:

● How are golden handshakes taxed?
● When is the best time to retire if you are self-employed?
● How is CGT charged on the sale of a business?

Working out your tax bill

There are two main taxes which may affect you: income tax and capital gains tax.

Income tax

We have set out the stages in the income tax computation in the form of a flow chart. There should be sufficient information for most people but in cases of unusual complexity it may be necessary to refer to the *Allied Dunbar Tax Guide* (ie if you have foreign domicile, or are a Lloyds Underwriter or own a farm etc). Employees with share options should take professional advice to ensure that any income tax charge on the exercise of the options is kept as low as possible.

Working out your tax liability

		Self	Wife	Tax paid
(1) *Compute earned income* National Insurance pension Occupational pension Retirement annuity Income from employment Freelance earnings	(i) (ii)			

Deduct retirement annuity relief (see p 96)

A

(2) *Compute investment income*		Self	Wife	Tax paid
National Savings Bank interest	(iii)			
Income from abroad	(iv)			
Income from property	(v)			
Dividends and taxed interest UK Bank and building society interest	(vi)			

B

(3) *Compute charges*		Self	Wife
Qualifying interest paid gross	(vii)		
Interest paid subject to MIRAS	(viii)		
Amount paid under charitable deeds of covenant	(ix)		

C

(4) *Compute other deductions*		
Business expansion scheme relief	(x)	
Allowable trading losses	(xi)	

D

Totals for self and wife

Total income (E)	A B	
Deduct	C & D E	

(5) *Compute personal allowances*

		Self	Wife
Single person's allowance	(xii)		
Married person's allowance	(xiii)		
Wife's earned income allowance	(xiv)		
	F		

(6) *Tax liability*

Basically one deducts F from E and applies the following tables. However note position on items in E which qualify only for higher rate relief, for example viii

0–17,900	27%
17,901–20,400	40%
20,401–25,400	45%
25,401–33,300	50%
33,301–41,200	55%
over 41,200	60%

Notes:

(i) Is this amount paid by virtue of the wife's own contributions? If so wife's earned income allowance is due.

(ii) This income will normally be assessable on the preceding year basis.

(iii) There is an exemption for the first £70 interest credited each year on the NSB ordinary account.

(iv) This income will normally be assessable on the preceding year basis.

(v) Does this include profits from furnished holiday accommodation? If so this counts as earned income.

(vi) The net amount received should be grossed up, ie net building society interest of £100 is grossed income of £136.98 (£100 × $\frac{100}{77}$). Enter grossed-up figure in B and tax figure (ie $\frac{3}{7}$) in tax paid column.

(vii) This interest can be deducted from your taxable income for all tax purposes.

(viii) Interest paid under MIRAS does not qualify for basic rate relief but should be taken into account if you are subject to higher rate tax.

(ix) The deed must require payments for a period of at least four years. Basic rate is deducted at source so these payments are relevant only if you are subject to higher rate tax.

(x) and (xi) See *Allied Dunbar Tax Guide.*

(xii) Basic allowance is £2,425. Age Allowance can increase this to £2,960 if income does not exceed £8,800.

(xiii) Basic allowance is £3,795. Age Allowance can increase this to £4,675.
Marginal Age Allowance can be claimed, the excess of taxable income over £9,800 results in a reduction of the allowance of £2 for every £3 excess income.

(xiv) Maximum relief is £2,425. The relief is limited to the amount of the wife's income if this is less.

How is age allowance computed?

Age relief consists of an increase in your personal allowance of £535 if you are single or £880 if you are married. You are eligible for the relief if you or your wife have attained age 65 at any time during the tax year. The relief is, however, also dependent on your taxable income not exceeding a certain limit. If your income exceeds £9,800 the extra allowance is reduced by £2 for every £3 of excess income.

Example

A has income of £9,920. The age addition to his personal allowance is therefore reduced by £80 ie 2/3rds of the income over the £9,800 limit.

Top slicing relief on investment bonds

Insurance bonds (see p 231) can be tax efficient investments — but you need to use them in the right way. A higher rate income tax charge may arise on their eventual disposal and this charge applies to the overall profit.

Example

A invests £10,000 in a bond on 1 January 1982. In March 1987 he cashes it in and receives £15,000. A's overall profit of £5,000 is not subject to the basic rate of 27% but is taxable at the higher rates if A is a higher rate tax payer because of his other income. Thus if A were subject to a top rate of tax of 45% there could be higher rate tax of 18% to pay on the profit of £5,000 (ie 45%–27%) so that tax of £900 would be payable.

Profits on the disposal of insurance bonds are normally an exceptional event and the tax legislation recognises this by giving top slicing relief. This is to enable gains to be 'spread' so that excessive tax is not payable because the exceptional income falls into just one year.

Example

Suppose that A's other income were such that only £3,000 of the £5,000 came within the 45% band and the £2,000 fell into the 40% band.

Before top slicing relief the tax payable would be:

2,000 at 13%	260
3,000 at 18%	540
	£800

When computing top slicing relief one divides the overall profit by the number of years that the policy has run, ie:

£5,000 divided by 5 = £1,000.

One then computes the extra tax found by adding that sum to A's other income, ie:

£1,000 at 13% = £130.

The tax on the £5,000 profit is £650, ie five (the number of policy years) X the tax on the notional amount of £1,000. The top slicing relief is therefore £150 (ie £800 less the actual tax liability of £650).

A similar tax charge can arise when amounts are taken out of a bond in excess of the tax free 5 per cent withdrawals. However, the computation is more complex and you should take professional advice.

Capital gains tax

Capital gains tax (CGT) is basically charged at 30 per cent on gains realised from the disposal of chargeable assets. Losses of a capital nature may generally be deducted in arriving at the chargeable amount.

There is normally no liability to CGT for transfers between husband and wife.

Your liability is worked out along the following lines:

See table overleaf

	Self	Wife
Gains on disposal of chargeable assets (see below)		
These are normally the net sale proceeds less cost		
Less indexation allowance	———	———
Less allowable losses on other disposals	———	———
Joint gains for year	———	
Less annual exemption	———	
Taxable at 30%	———	

Chargeable assets

A chargeable gain may arise on the disposal of any asset, other than an asset which is specifically exempt for CGT purposes. The following assets are regarded as exempt from CGT:

- *Dwelling houses* — an individual is exempt from CGT insofar as he realises a gain on a property which has been his only or main residence or the only or main residence of a dependent relative.
- *Chattels* — a tangible, moveable asset is entirely exempt provided that the disposal proceeds do not exceed £3,000.
- *Gilts* — Government securities and most corporate loan stocks are exempt from CGT. The position needs to be looked at more closely where company loan stocks were held prior to 14 March 1984.
- *Debts* — no CGT normally arises on a disposal of a debt unless it is a 'debt on a security'. A debt on a security is normally a transferable debt such as a loan stock.

In practice capital gains would not normally arise on the disposal of a debt and it is more probable that a capital loss would arise. Because debts are exempt assets for CGT purposes, no relief is normally available for losses which arise from the disposal of debts other than debts on a security.

● *Foreign currency* — this is exempt provided that it was acquired for the owner's personal expenditure abroad. This includes the provision or maintenance of a residence abroad.

● *Insurance policies* — the original owner of an insurance policy is not subject to CGT on the proceeds. You are also exempt if you were given the policy.

● *Motor cars* — a vehicle constructed or adapted for the carriage of passengers is exempt from CGT unless it is a vehicle of a type not commonly used as a private vehicle and unsuitable to be so used.

● *Savings certificates* — National Saving Certificates and other similar securities are not chargeable assets for CGT purposes.

Main residence exemption

In practice, most people are mainly concerned about the position on the disposal of their main residence and the flow chart overleaf should make the position clear.

Sale of a company or business

It is more difficult to avoid CGT on the sale of a business. By the very nature of things, a purchaser will wish there to be continuity of trading and will not just be acquiring assets which are used in a trade. Indeed, there will often be a significant element of goodwill in the price, and this definitely requires continuity. The problem is that a vendor will not be able to avoid CGT by deferring a sale until he has ceased to be UK resident.

Allowable deductions

We must now examine the deductions which may be claimed.

Indexation allowance This is an allowance to compensate for the inflation which has occurred since 31 March 1982. The allowance is computed by the formula $\frac{RD-RI}{RI}$ where:

RD = the RPI for the month of disposal.
RI = the RPI for the month of acquisition, or March 1982 (if later).

Sale of main residence

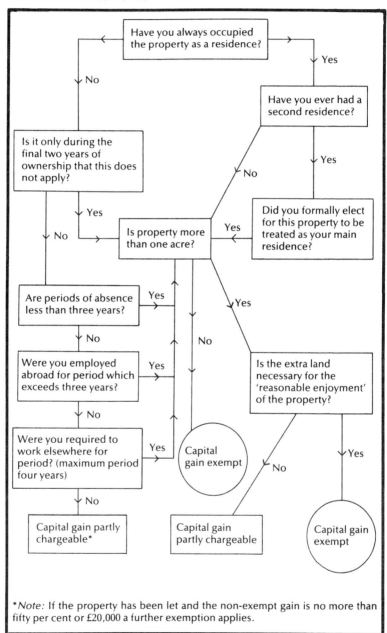

Note: If the property has been let and the non-exempt gain is no more than fifty per cent or £20,000 a further exemption applies.

Example

C sells shares for £30,000.
They cost £10,000 in 1969.
The RPI for the month of disposal is 390.
The RPI for March 1982 was 313.4.
He can claim indexation allowance of:

$$\frac{390 - 313.4}{313.4} \times 10,000 = £746$$

and this is treated as a deduction in computing the chargeable gain.

An election may be made to claim the indexation allowance on the value of the asset at 31 March 1982.

Example

Suppose the shares had been worth £25,000 in March 1982.
C's indexation allowance would then be *£1,865.*

An election needs to be made within two years of the end of the year of disposal. Once made the election is irrevocable. It may be difficult to ascertain the market value at 31 March 1982 when land or unquoted shares are involved and careful thought should be given to the situation before an election is made.

Annual exemption Another allowable item is the 'annual exemption'. This is presently £6,600. Note that the £6,600 is deducted from your capital gains and no unused part of the £6,600 can be carried forward. Also bear in mind that there is only one annual exemption for a married couple.

The detailed CGT rules are very complicated and you may need to consult the *Allied Dunbar Tax Guide*. If you dispose of almost anything other than your main residence and quoted stocks and shares you may be well advised to consult a solicitor or accountant.

Tax planning

The first part of this chapter has been descriptive, we now focus on some tax planning aspects:

Choosing the right retirement date

It can make quite a lot of difference whether you retire at the beginning or end of a tax year. One situation where timing can be crucial is where a person receives a golden handshake on retirement. To understand this it is necessary to go into some detail on the way in which golden handshakes and compensation payments are taxed.

Golden handshakes and compensation payments are known to the Inland Revenue as 'termination payments'. They are treated as income which arises at the date the employment terminates. It therefore makes no difference that the actual payment may be delayed until the next tax year; if A's employment ceased on 31 March 1987, his golden handshake is assessed for 1986/87 even though it may be paid on 6 April 1987 or later during the tax year 1987/88.

A golden handshake is taxable in full as income if the director/employee is entitled to it under his contract of employment. In other cases there is an exemption for the first £25,000. This exemption applies whether the payment is expressed to be *ex-gratia* or a compensation payment.

For the sake of completeness, it should also be mentioned that statutory redundancy payments are not themselves taxable, but they do consume part of the £25,000 exemption.

Example

B receives compensation of £20,000 and statutory redundancy payments of £8,000. The redundancy payments are exempt, but mean that part of the compensation is taxable:

Compensation		£20,000
Exemption	£25,000	
Less	£ 8,000	£17,000
Taxable amount		£3,000

Top slicing relief

A further relief is given in the form of a reduction in the rate of tax. The tax charged on the first £25,000 chargeable (ie after deducting the exemption) is at 50 per cent of the rate which would otherwise be payable and the next £25,000 is charged at 75 per cent of the normal rate.

Example

If C receives a golden handshake of £40,000 and had other taxable income (after allowances) in that year of £28,000 the tax payable on the £15,000 which is taxable would be computed as follows:

Total taxable income	*£43,000* tax thereon	£17,458
Deduct tax payable on other income	£28,000	9,383
		8,075

Tax actually payable on the £40,000 compensation is 50% of £8,075 ie £4,037.50.

Timing of retirement

It should now be obvious that the best time to terminate an employment is at the very start of a tax year if your marginal rate of tax will be lower after retirement. The effects of the top-slicing relief will often be to eliminate tax on a golden hand-shake if you retire on 6 April.

There is also a planning point for the self-employed. Your retirement may give rise to a cessation for Schedule D purposes (see *Allied Dunbar Tax Guide*) and this means that the Inland Revenue may be able to increase your tax assessments for the two years preceding the year of your retirement. In some cases it may be worth deferring your retirement until shortly after 5 April, so as to limit the extent of the Inland Revenue's adjustments for past years.

The Revenue's powers arise from the fact that self-employed earnings are assessed on the preceding year basis. The Revenue are permitted to tax your actual earnings for the year of cessation and to adjust the assessments for the two full tax years preceding the year of retirement if this results in an overall increase (the Revenue cannot just adjust one year in isolation).

Example

A is self-employed and has an accounting date of 30 June. His profits and tax assessments have been as follows:

		Assessed tax year
Year ended 30 June 1984	£15,000	1985/86
Year ended 30 June 1985	£20,000	1986/87
Year ended 30 June 1986	£25,000	1987/88

If A retires on 5 April 1988 and his last two years' results were £30,000 (year ended 30 June 1987) and £15,000 (nine month period ended 5 April 1988) the Revenue would replace the 1987/88 assessment with the actual earnings for the year of £22,500 (ie 3 × 12 profits for the year to 30 June 1987 + the profits for the final nine months) and the two preceding years would be adjusted as follows:

1985/86:	3/12 × profits for year ended 30 June 1985	5,000
	9/12 × profits for year ended 30 June 1986	18,750
		23,750

1986/87:	3/12 × profits for year ended 30 June 1986	6,250
	9/12 × profits for year ended 30 June 1987	22,500
		28,750

Thus additional income would be assessed for 1985/86 of £8,750 and a similar adjustment made for 1986/87.

If A delayed his retirement until 6 April 1988, the Revenue could not adjust 1985/86 and the adjustments for the two following years would not be so great in total.

It is important to take professional advice on such a matter as the timing of a cessation. Special provisions apply where a person has been a member of a partnership.

CGT on the sale of your business/private company

This is another area where the timing of your retirement may be very important. Even if you cannot avoid payments of CGT, it would obviously be more beneficial to dispose of your business/company on 6 April rather than 5 April. The additional delay in the payment of CGT for 12 months can be very valuable in these times of high interest rates.

It may, on the other hand, be possible to reduce the liability if the gain can be deferred until such time as you are entitled to the full CGT retirement relief.

This relief is available broadly speaking in the following circumstances:

(a)   the person realising the gain must be at least 60 or be forced to retire because of ill-health;
(b)   the person must have been engaged in the trade or have been a full-time working director of a family trading company;
(c)   the gain must arise on the sale of the business or shares in the family company or of an asset owned by the person but used rent free (or at a rent lower than the commercial rent) by the business or company.

The maximum relief is available only if the person has carried on business or been a full-time working director for the ten years preceding the disposal.

Both husband and wife can qualify for the full £125,000 relief if they meet the necessary conditions (for further details on this see *Allied Dunbar Tax Guide*).

The way in which the relief operates is complex and professional advice should be taken, but in principle you should time a disposal on retirement so as to ensure that full advantage is taken of the relief. All other things being equal it may pay to carry on another year rather than retire at (say) age 59 and pay substantial amounts of CGT.

How can you minimise tax in the year of retirement?
One possibility that is often overlooked is to pay pension premiums.

Last minute pension contributions
As you draw close to retirement it is worth considering whether additional voluntary contributions or personal pension contributions can be paid. Even though the money may be with the insurance company for a relatively short time, the fact that the contributions attract income tax relief and a lump sum may be taken tax-free means that there is often substantial advantage in paying such contributions.

Checklist for year of retirement

● Will it be beneficial to defer the date of your retirement because you will receive a golden handshake?

● If you are self-employed, can you mitigate the tax consequences of a cessation of business on your retirement?

● Take advice on the sale of your private business or family company so as to minimise any capital gains tax.

● Can you pay further personal pension premiums?

11 Carry on working

Many people are reluctant to give up work completely and choose to continue on a part-time basis. This raises several questions:

● How much can you earn without affecting your state pension?
● What happens if you defer taking your state pension?
● What happens if you do not draw your company pension right away?
● How will your part-time earnings be assessed for tax purposes and what is the National Insurance position?
● What can you do to save tax?

How much can you earn without affecting your state pension?

In principle you can continue to work part-time and draw the state pension. However, this is not just a matter of taking a reduction in your salary. What is also important is the overall type of work. If you have not substantially changed your working hours, then it will be difficult for you to claim that you have actually retired and you will not therefore be eligible for a pension.

Working on a part-time basis after age 65 will not result in a restriction of the state pension unless you earn more than £75 per week. Once earnings rise above this level the basic state retirement pension is progressively reduced and if earnings exceed £138 per week the pension is lost altogether by a married man. For a single person the sum is only £116 a week before the pension is lost. In the case of a wife over 60 who draws the pension of £23.25 per week, earnings of £100 per week or more will be sufficient to completely stop the pension. Where a husband is retired but has a working wife under the age of 60 he can claim the £23.25 per week extra pension for her. However, if she earns more than £30.80 a week (including any occupational pension) then the extra pension will stop. Once she attains the age of 60 and draws a pension in her own right then any reduction in the pension will be applied in the usual way.

For these purposes one looks at gross earnings before tax but after National Insurance contributions. One can also deduct the cost of items such as:

● trade union subscriptions
● fares to and from work
● cost of tools and other equipment.

When applying these restrictions, no account is taken of income from occupational pensions (except as mentioned above), nor are investment income or savings taken into account.

Happily, once a man attains the age of 70, or a woman age 65, they can earn as much as they like without this affecting their pension.

What happens if you defer taking your state pension?

It may be that if you are working, say, three days a week you can afford to defer drawing your pension. This may enable the pension to be increased substantially when you eventually start to take it. The state pension can, in fact, be deferred until age 70. Deferring the pension results in its being increased by approximately 7.5 per cent per annum. Over five years this means that the pension is increased by a third — in addition to any inflation adjustments.

What happens if you do not draw your company pension right away?

In some cases, especially where you have an executive pension scheme (sometimes known as an individual pension arrangement) it is possible to defer taking the pension and this can be a sensible way to proceed because of the tax free nature of the pension fund.

Similarly, if you have made additional voluntary contributions you may be able to draw the benefits under the main pension scheme but defer the benefits funded under the AVC scheme.

Unfortunately, if you are a member of the large group scheme there is often less scope for manoeuvre. It may be that the choices open to you are simply either to retire and start drawing your pension or to carry on working. This is something that you should investigate, probably via your company's personnel department.

How will your part-time earnings be assessed for tax purposes?

The position will vary according to whether you are employed or self-employed. This will normally depend upon whether you are working on a part-time basis for a single employer or are working on a freelance basis for several different customers — although other considerations may also be relevant. In some cases the distinction may be difficult to draw and you would be well advised to obtain a copy of the Inland Revenue leaflet *Employed or self-employed?*

If you are employed then your earnings will be taxed under the PAYE system. You may well have your code number amended to reflect the fact that you are drawing your state pension. Your taxable earnings will be those which arise during the year. There are very few allowable expenses.

If you are self-employed your taxable earnings will normally be assessed on the preceding year basis. This is the normal basis of assessment for a self-employed person and means that the income for a tax year is taken to be the profits of his accounts which end in the preceding tax year.

Example

A draws up his accounts to 30 June. His profits for the year ended 30 June 1986 will determine the tax assessment for 1987/88.

Starting a new business

A special rule applies when a person starts a new business. His profits for the first tax year are based upon his actual earnings from the date he commenced his business to the following 5 April. For the second tax year he is assessed on his earnings for the first 12 months of trading.

Example

A starts a business on 1 January 1987, with an accounting year end 31.12.87.

His results are as follows:

Year ended 31 December 1987	£6,000
Year ended 31 December 1988	£12,000
Year ended 31 December 1989	£15,000

The tax assessments would be:

1986/87 3/12 × £6,000 (ie profits from 1.1.87 to 5.4.87)	£1,500
1987/88 first 12 months	£6,000
1988/89 preceding year basis	£6,000
1989/90 preceding year basis	£12,000

The basis of assessment suits A here as he is assessed on a total of £13,500 whereas his actual earnings for the period amounted to £33,000! However, if it had been the other way round A could elect for his tax assessments for his second and third year to be based on his actual profits. Note that the election can only be made by the taxpayer and that it cannot be made for one year in isolation.

Note also that there are closing year rules for when a business ceases and this could mean a heavier tax liability to counterbalance the lower liability in the opening year.

National Insurance contributions

National Insurance contributions will not be payable by you after retirement but if you are employed you may still be liable for contributions.

How can you save tax?

The rules on what expenses are allowable are much easier if you are self-employed — especially if you work from home. An employed person has to show that expenses have been incurred 'wholly, exclusively and necessarily' in performing the duties of the employment. A self-employed person need only show that they were incurred 'wholly and exclusively' for business purposes. You should for example be able to claim for:

- travelling expenses (not to and from your office to home),
- postage and stationery,
- telephone, heat and light, and
- possibly a payment to your wife for secretarial work.

These are things which you should discuss with an accountant, together with matters such as:

- Can you claim expenses for using part of your home for business purposes?
- What other expenses will be allowable?
- Will you need to register for VAT purposes?

There are two other tax planning points which are worthy of special mention: choosing the right accounting date and paying private pension contributions.

Choosing the right accounting date

One idea is to draw up accounts to 30 April so as to take full advantage of the preceding year basis (this assumes that profits will be increasing year by year).

Example

B starts a business on 1 January 1987. His first accounts are for a period of one year and four months, ie up to 30 April 1988. Suppose his actual profits are:

First 16 months	£8,000
Year to 30 April 1988	10,000
Year to 30 April 1989	12,000
Year to 30 April 1990	15,000
	45,000

(*continued overleaf*)

His taxable income may well be much less and will usually be worked out as follows:

1986/87	3/16 × £8,000 (ie profits to 5.4.87)	£1,500
1987/88	12/16 × £8,000 (ie first twelve months profits)	6,000
1988/89	12/16 × £8,000 (ie on the same basis as 1987/88)	6,000
1989/90	Preceding year basis	6,000
		£19,500

Try to keep your taxable profits for the first year down to the minimum as this increases the benefit under the preceding year basis of assessment. In some cases it may be worth starting up in business with your wife as an employee and bringing her into partnership after the first 12 months.

Paying into a private pension plan

If you decide to draw your company pension and work part-time, don't forget that your part-time earnings will be non-pensionable earnings. Accordingly, you can obtain tax relief for personal pension premiums. These can offer an excellent return.

Example

A 71 year old man with part-time earnings of £5,000 could obtain tax relief for 'one-off' personal pension premiums of £1,000. The pension policy might provide for a lump sum and annuity to be taken from age 73. Assuming a marginal rate of tax of 55% the figures might work out like this:

retirement annuity premium	£1,000
less tax relief	550
net cost	450
less tax free lump sum	389
	(61)

The amount which may be taken as a tax free lump sum may be slightly less for pension policies effected after 31 December 1987, but the on-going pension will be correspondingly increased.

This exercise would currently result in an on-going pension of around £106 per annum — leaving the individual in a profit position after only 1 year!

12 Managing your money

Even if you have the maximum pension, there will still be some reduction in your income at the very time that you have more opportunity to enjoy the things that money can buy. Furthermore, the gap between your pension and your expenditure is likely to grow because of inflation. This is where your savings come in: invested judiciously they will produce the extra income that you need and bridge the gap between your expenditure and pension to maintain your income as you grow older.

The next chapters deal with the following questions:

- What are the main criteria to use when evaluating an investment?
- What type of investments are available?
  This section is descriptive rather than prescriptive and sets out the main features of various types of investments such as building society deposits, gilts, unit trusts etc.
- What guiding principles should you follow when you plan your portfolio?

What are the main criteria to use when evaluating an investment?

There is a vast variety of different kinds of investment from which to choose. Each has its own particular advantages and drawbacks. You want to choose those which can give you the greatest number of important advantages while incurring the fewest significant disadvantages. The choice depends both on your circumstances and your temperament, so that an investment which is attractive for one person may be quite unsuitable for another. Clearly age has a great deal to do with an investor's 'perspective': as you get older, income may be more important than capital growth. Guaranteed return may become more desirable, and so on.

It is of paramount importance to define clearly your personal investment priorities and then decide which investment or investments best suit your circumstances.

A simple illustration of this is the choice which you get from a bank. It is no good putting money into a deposit account subject to one month's notice if you want to use it to pay bills this week. On the other hand, most current accounts do not pay you interest. What you need is sufficient in your current account to cover day to day needs, while any surplus is kept on deposit. In this way you get the best of both worlds.

As an alternative, 'high interest' bank accounts are becoming more and more popular. These are effectively interest bearing current accounts with the full range of cheque book and other typical banking facilities. Some also have built-in credit card and temporary loan facilities.

These types of account are a vital part of financial planning. This is where you should keep the money that you need to be able to get at in a hurry — either to pay a bill or to take advantage of a sudden opportunity (which could mean a holiday and not just an investment).

With long-term investment however, the position is different. This is cash which is not needed now but which will probably be needed in the future, either as a capital sum to cover a large item of expediture or for re-investment to produce an income. Therefore, the most important requirement for this money is that it at least retains its real value (ie in terms of what it will buy) and, ideally, it will actually increase its real value over a period of time.

It is, of course, difficult to know exactly where this money should be placed. Today's investor is approached from all sides with an almost bewildering array of investment choices. The financial columns of the daily newspapers and the ever increasing number of financial magazines are packed with suggestions on where the investor should place his or her money — with the suggestions frequently being backed-up with impressive graphs and statistics.

There are more than thirty different kinds of investment commonly used by ordinary people. Some of the categories contain hundreds or even thousands of different choices. There are now more than 1,000 unit trusts being actively promoted, and several new ones are started almost every week.

Personal circumstances

Choosing an investment is not simply a matter of deciding how you can make the most of your money. It is not even a matter of choosing the investment that will produce the most money when you need it. In 1986 the ordinary share index on the London Stock Market moved up by some 25 per cent. This was obviously pleasing to most investors. The fact remains that the progress was not even. It rose sharply for the first four months of the year; in the summer, prices drifted downwards. Since October when important changes occurred at the Stock Exchange (Big Bang) there have been sharp short-term fluctuations. As a whole the market in December was still substantially higher than at the start of the year but this masks a wide variety of performance with some individual stocks showing large losses.

At times like this of course it is important to take a long-term view of investment management. It is only too easy to judge the success of an investment or groups of investments by recent performance without appreciating the risks that are inherent in following any form of aggressive investment policy, particularly when the stock markets of the world have had a history of sustained growth since 1975. For the average investor, a typical investment philosophy could well be summed up in the Allied Dunbar approach to investment. This approach aims to protect investors against *avoidable* risks. It is based upon a *responsible* approach to investment by pointing out that no investment group can consistently pick winners no matter how experienced they may be, and advising most strongly that nobody should rely upon short-term investment performance (or selective investment performance) as a guide to the future. When looking for the right home for your long-term savings, it's important to avoid extravagant claims because the most important concern for most people is that they should be able to protect their hard-earned savings and to obtain a consistent above average return.

An important principle of the Allied Dunbar approach is therefore one of protection and the company believes that there are three principal aspects of this in relation to investment:

(1)   Protection against inflation is achieved in the long term through investing in shares and properties which are asset-backed investments and which offer the best long-term *prospects* of growth and real return.
(2)   Protection through spread can be achieved through investing in a range of equities, properties and gilt-edged securities on, in the case of equities, a worldwide basis. Furthermore, equities can be spread across different sectors and within sectors across different companies, thereby minimising the risk of an unexpectedly poor performance of a single investment.
(3)   Protection through relying upon experts is achieved by using the skills, sources of information, back-up and judgment of full-time fund managers.

For the great majority of people, their investment needs will be satisfied through investing in a managed investment fund (p 166) or in a selective portfolio of unit trusts (p 160). Having done this, they should have no need to worry about switching from one form of investment to another, or about changes in currency, or about which world economies are performing better or worse.

It's at this point that you have to determine your own approach to investment. By its very nature, a managed investment fund or a portfolio of unit trusts sets out to contain risk, and it does this by spreading the total investment across a wide range of individual stocks and shares. Consequently, it is unlikely to show the dramatic growth of individual shares but nor is it so vulnerable to the rapid falls which are possible. There would be nothing unusual in the price of an individual share going up by a factor of three or more in a twelve month period; it would be an untypical performance that consistently lifted the price of a unit trust by a third over the same period.

In choosing a managed fund or portfolio of unit trusts you

must sacrifice the potential for startling growth in return for greater security. Only you can decide whether you wish to hold potentially volatile investments. Normally, they will produce better returns than those which fluctuate less — provided you're prepared to take the risks. Indeed, one of the classic ways of increasing your return is by choosing volatile investments which are affected by differing factors. If you get it right, the rises in some will offset the falls in others and you will benefit over the long-term and the higher rate of return given to comparatively risky investments. Unfortunately, it is difficult to be sure that investments will move in different directions. They may all move up — but there's always the risk that they may all move down.

Analysis

There are a number of ways of looking at investments. Some of them are helpful, whereas others tell you more about the person who uses them than the investment itself. One of the most valuable ones grades them according to the degree of risk involved. At one end of the spectrum lies cash, which in theory carries no risk, but which of course also offers no chance of capital appreciation. At the other extreme are such things as commodity futures, or a bet on an outsider in the 3.30. Here the chances are that you will lose your money, but if you win, the benefit will be very great indeed. In theory at least, it is possible to give a position on this scale to every type of investment.

Another way of grading investments is according to their liquidity. Liquidity simply means how quickly an investment can be turned into cash. Money in your pocket or a current account at a bank can be put at one end of the scale. At the other end of the scale are investments like property which can take time to sell. The assessment of liquidity is complicated by the fact that many illiquid investments can be used as security for a loan.

Traditionally these two measures were all that investors needed. The more risky or illiquid an investment was thought to be, the higher the potential return it offered. Sometimes the market would overestimate the risk attached to an investment which made it possible to obtain a relatively high return with comparatively little risk. Investment is primarily a matter of determining what risks you are able to run and how much liquidity you need.

These measures are valid, but their assessment is greatly complicated by two factors. These are tax and inflation, both of which became increasingly important as the twentieth century went by. The last few years have seen both of them become less significant but it remains to be seen whether the change is permanent. Even if it is, both price rises and taxation remain much higher than they were 20 or 25 years ago.

Tax

Investments are taxed in different ways, depending upon their nature. The higher your tax rate, the more important this is. An investment which is appropriate for a person paying little tax may be unattractive to someone who pays tax at the higher rates.

Let us look at building society investment. At the time of writing, a 90 day investment share pays 9 per cent with basic rate tax paid. This to the ordinary man is slightly better than the 11.75 per cent gross which is payable on a National Savings investment account. After allowing for tax at 27 per cent, the return on the National Savings investments is only 8.57 per cent. In contrast, however, a man who pays no tax at all would have done much better with the investment account, since he cannot reclaim the tax which the building society has paid. At the other extreme is the 6 per cent tax free which is paid on ordinary accounts of over £500 with the National Savings Bank up to a total interest of £70 per annum. This is not attractive to the man who pays no tax, and is outbid by the building society for the basic rate taxpayer. On the other hand, the man who pays tax at 60 per cent on any additional income will find the 6 per cent better than the 4.94 per cent which he will get after paying tax on the grossed up interest from the building society.

There is a simple rule for dealing with tax — always work out what the net return will be for you after tax. This is all that matters. Advertisements often like to quote gross yields. This is understandable, since the figures are much larger. Unfortunately, most of us will only receive our income after paying tax on it.

The taxation of capital gains, however, is much simpler. Everyone who makes a capital gain on their investment pays the same rate of tax. You will be taxed at the rate of 30 per cent on realised gains, but only after taking into account the following allowance:

(a) *The annual allowance* The first £6,600 of your net gains for 1987/88 are exempted from tax. The amount of the allowance is generally increased each year in line with increases in the cost of living. Note, however, that a married couple receive only one allowance between them.
(b) Most capital losses which you realise can be deducted in arriving at your chargeable capital gains.
(c) *Indexation* A deduction can be made from the gain to take account of the effects of inflation; also any loss that you make can be increased.
(d) Certain assets that produce capital gains are exempt from CGT, ie Government Stock and National Savings Certificates.

Clearly, the taxation of capital gains is much more favourable than the profits or income derived from interest bearing investments. It is, therefore, sensible when planning your investments to take account of the differences in taxation so as to ensure that you suffer the lowest overall rate of tax. However, investment return is the most important requirement, you should never let the 'tax tail wag the investment dog'.

Inflation

Until recently, inflation faced investors with an unwelcome choice. If they selected very secure investments to safeguard their capital, they faced the certainty that it would be gradually eroded as the purchasing power of money declined. If, on the other hand, they chose less secure investments whose value was likely to increase to compensate for inflation, they ran the risk of suffering a loss. The traditional inflation hedges of shares and property are well known for the fact that their value can go down as well as up.

The chief sufferers from this were the small investors who were dependent upon their savings. As a result, it was to these people that the remedy of index linking was first made available. Unfortunately, the original index linked investments, granny bonds, were not particularly attractive. Despite this, large sums of money were put into them as their availability was widened. More recently, a much more attractive inflation protected investment has been made available in the form of index linked gilts. Initially, however, they could only be bought by pension funds. After a year the restriction was removed, and everyone is now free to buy index linked government stock. The result has been to give everyone the opportunity of complete protection against inflation. The potential of this is clearly very great, but so far few private investors have taken advantage of the opportunity.

Although inflation has receded as a threat, it certainly has not disappeared, and could easily re-emerge as the dominant investment consideration. Between 1976 and 1982, prices doubled. This meant that if your investment did not grow by more than 100 per cent, you actually got poorer. As in 'Alice Through The Looking Glass', it took all the running you could do to stay in the same place. If you want to get somewhere else, you must run twice as fast as that.

If prices are stable, cash represents a safe investment. In an inflationary world, this is not so. A pound tomorrow will be worth less than a pound today. Even the present rate of 5 per cent can have a serious effect: inflation at 5 per cent for ten years means that unless your capital has grown in value by 63 per cent you are actually poorer. In the past, of course, things have been much worse. During the ten years to 1982 prices rose 200 per cent, and at the end of the period things cost three and a half times as much as they did in 1970. In other words, in 1982 you needed one pound to buy what could be purchased for 5s 11d in 1970. Some things have gone up even more. A London evening paper in 1970 cost 6d (2½p), while its successor in 1986 costs 20p — an increase of 800 per cent over 16 years. Although this appears an enormous increase, it actually represents an average rate of inflation of only 15 per cent. It takes very few years of double digit inflation to increase prices several hundred per cent.

There is no complete solution to the problem of inflation where the rate of price increases outstrips the return you can obtain on your investments. It is therefore important to ensure that, to as great a degree as possible, your investments are arranged in such a way as to produce the best return while retaining sufficient flexibility in order that they can be adapted to changing investment and inflationary conditions.

The next few chapters describe the main features of various different types of investment.

13 Interest bearing investments

By 'interest bearing investments' we mean those investments where the return is governed by interest rates. This covers a broad range of investments. In some cases the capital value is fixed but the interest may fluctuate; in other cases, the reverse applies. In yet other cases the return varies according to inflation. However, whilst there is a variety, the basic feature of these investments is that they are not 'risk' investments. We start by looking at fixed capital investments.

Whatever your circumstances, you need to keep at least a part of your assets in some form of fixed capital investment, even if it is only a comparatively small reserve for the proverbial rainy day. There is a great variety of this type of investment, but these types can be narrowed down to a few which offer the best solutions for the great majority of investors, and that are applicable to most investors, and we outline those that are most commonly used by the public as a home for their savings.

Building societies

The most basic building society investment is the ordinary share. The great attraction of this is that you can lay your hands on your money whenever you want it. In addition, it pays a competitive rate of interest. On the other hand, it is not at all appropriate for a person who pays no income tax at all, since he cannot reclaim the tax which the building society has paid. Although building society ordinary shares are popular, they are not necessarily the best place for retired people to keep a significant part of their capital. If you can put in the money so that it is subject to 90 days' notice of withdrawal, you may earn as much as 3 per cent per annum extra interest over the ordinary share rate. In practice you are highly unlikely to need a large sum of money without any warning. Even if you do, the penalties are relatively modest, the loss of 90 days' interest may be outweighed by the extra interest that you have earned in the past few years. As a result, the advantage of immediate accessibility is of little use to retired people. They can do much better by tying their money up for a little longer.

Until recently, the terms offered by building societies were all much the same, although a few of the smaller ones offered slightly higher rates. Today, the situation has become much more competitive and it certainly makes sense to look around before deciding where to place your money. Once you have chosen a society you should regularly review the market in order to make sure that you can't do better elsewhere. A number of newspapers and financial magazines publish surveys of building society investments from time to time. It is still generally true that the best terms are available from some of the smaller specialist societies. They are able to offer them because they tend to provide higher priced mortgages.

Certain investors shy away from putting money with a small society. It is doubtful whether this is a sensible reaction if it is a member of the Building Societies Association. In the past, when one of the members has got into trouble, the others have rallied round and protected the investors from loss.

Government stock

Government stock, or 'gilts', are also a very attractive form of interest bearing investments but they are also one of the least used by the private investor. Perhaps this is because they can seem complicated compared to other interest bearing investments. There are a large number of different issues of government stock, each with its own unique characteristics. Most of them are due to be redeemed either on a fixed date or within a certain period of time. The attraction for the Government of having a certain amount of latitude over the timing is that it can choose to redeem the stock when conditions are favourable. If it is tied to a fixed date, the money must be repaid regardless of the circumstances. The stock is normally denominated in units of £100 (known as the 'nominal' or 'par' value) and this is the amount which will be repaid on redemption.

Every stock pays interest and this is normally done every six months. The rate of interest varies greatly from one issue to another. Some stock is known as having a 'high coupon', and pays a high rate of interest such as 10, 11 or 12 per cent whereas other issues are known as 'low coupon' stocks and these may pay out 3, 4 or 5 per cent.

As well as differences in the interest rate, the stocks have different redemption dates. Some are due to be repaid within a matter of months whereas others won't be until well into the next century. Stocks with less than five years to redemption are generally known as 'shorts' and those with between five and fifteen years are known as 'medium'. Over fifteen years defines a 'long'. There are even a few issues of 'undated' stock which may never be redeemed.

Government stocks are traded on the Stock Exchange and their value is liable to fluctuate. Clearly, the value of any one stock is unlikely to be far from the par value of £100 when it is close to its redemption date. On the other hand, if redemption is many years in the future the value of the stock can fluctuate considerably as interest rates move up and down.

When other interest rates are high the price of government stocks will be low in value so as to produce a matching compatible return. Conversely, as rates fall, the stock value will rise. The greatest fluctuations are seen in undated stock and those with redemption dates which are far in the future. For this reason, those who wish to minimise the risks they are running are well advised to restrict their investments to the short dated issues which are conventionally taken to be those whose redemption is no more than five years ahead.

The prices of gilt edged stock are shown in the leading newspapers and beside them will be shown different figures indicating the return which is available to an investor. These may differ from the nominal interest which the stock pays. The reason for this is that the price is likely to be considerably removed from the par value of £100. It may be either higher or lower. If it is below par value when it is bought and held right up to redemption the holder can expect to receive a capital gain in addition to the income that will be paid on the stock. Set out below are examples of several typical issues:

Government stocks—redemption yields
Annual returns after tax deductions (where applicable)

	No tax	27%	40%	50%	60%
Shorts					
Treasury 3% 1987 (85 3/8)	9.67	8.79	8.36	8.03	7.71
Treasury 12% 1987 (101 13/16)	11.23	7.81	6.18	4.92	3.67
Mediums					
Treasury 13% 1990 (105 7/8)	11.32	8.00	6.36	5.11	3.87
Funding 5 3/4% 1987/91 (82 1/4)	9.94	8.09	7.20	6.52	5.84
Longs					
Treasury 13 3/4% 2000/3 (118 5/16)	11.14	7.87	6.33	5.12	3.89
Funding $3\frac{1}{2}$% 1999/2004 (47 3/4)	9.37	7.79	7.07	6.51	5.96

The first stock shown, Treasury 3 per cent 1987, would cost £85 $\frac{3}{8}$ for every £100 'nominal'. This will provide an income of £3 a year ie interest of 3.51 per cent on the purchase price.

In addition, the buyer will receive a guaranteed £100 sometime in 1987 (the actual redemption date varies with the stock: in this case it happens to be 14 July 1987). The increase in value from £85 $\frac{3}{8}$ to £100 can clearly be expressed as an annual rate of growth and this when combined with the 3.51 per cent interest equates to an overall investment return of 9.67 per cent gross — the 'redemption' yield.

The £3 is taxable as income and so the net yield at different tax rates is also shown. Capital gains on gilts are not taxable.

The next stock will also be redeemed in 1987. In this case, however, the stock pays a higher level of income and the price of the stock reflects this. Anybody buying this stock is looking purely for income because they will incur a capital loss if they hold on to it until redemption.

This produces a higher return for non taxpayers but a lower one for those paying tax. The reason for this is that the two returns from the investment are taxed differently. Income from government stock is taxed in exactly the same way as from any other source. Capital gains, in contrast, are tax free. As a result, there is a considerable demand from high rate taxpayers for stock which stands at a discount from its redemption value and will in consequence produce a tax free capital gain rather than income.

A similar pattern exists with the longer dated issues. After a time the prospect of redemption ceases to have any real effect on the stock's price, all that matters is the income which it produces. These stocks and, in particular, the undated issues are bought by those who believe that interest rates are likely to fall so that they can be sold in order to make a capital gain. In the meantime, they enjoy the comparatively high income. Thus the funding $3\frac{1}{2}$ per cent standing at £47 $\frac{3}{4}$ produces annual gross income of 7.32 per cent on the money invested in contrast to less than half this rate from the short dated stock.

Index-linked government stock

Public interest was limited when index-linked gilts were originally introduced. One reason for this was that the private investor was not able to buy them. This was quickly changed but they were less attractive since inflation was falling. There are now no less than 12 different index-linked government stocks with redemption dates ranging from 1988 to 2020.

The index-linked government stock or 'gilts' work in exactly the same way as conventional gilts except that the nominal value and the interest payments are adjusted to take account of the fall in the value of money. The adjustment effectively increases their value by the rise in the Retail Price Index. The value of this naturally depends much upon the future rate of inflation. If it is low then the value of the inflation protection is small. If the economy does less well and inflation is high, it will be correspondingly enhanced.

Although the nominal value and the interest are index linked this does not mean that the security will retain the same real value all the time. It is traded on the Stock Exchange and its price will vary according to demand, just as that of any other government stock does. However, if you buy stock and hold it to redemption you know exactly what return you will get in terms of real purchasing power.

If you sell it in the interim, you may do either better or worse, depending upon how the market has moved in the meantime. During the few years this stock has been in existence, it has been much less affected by changes in interest rates than are conventional gilts. At the present price levels all the index linked stocks promise a running yield (annual income) of around $2\frac{1}{4}$–$2\frac{3}{4}$ per cent on top of any index linking. Allowing for the addition capital gain to redemption, real returns vary from a total of over 4 per cent on the shortest stocks to 3 per cent on the longer issues.

It is difficult to compare an index-linked investment with a conventional one. It all depends on what the rate of inflation will be in the future, and this cannot be forecast accurately. If you are interested in putting some of your money into this sort of investment you may need to get expert advice.

Off-shore roll-up funds

We have previously mentioned how these operate (p 102) and the way in which the tax bill is deferred until the investor realises his investment. These funds are for all practical purposes the equivalent of having money on deposit in the Isle of Man and the Channel Islands and the tax treatment can make them most attractive. An investor could, for example, use an investment in such a fund to take an annual 'income', much of which could be tax free.

Example

An investor has £100,000 in a sterling fund which achieves growth of 12% per annum. If £12,000 is drawn off each year the following amounts will be subject to income tax:

Year 1	1285	Year 6	5921
Year 2	2434	Year 7	6572
Year 3	3459	Year 8	7154
Year 4	4374	Year 9	7673
Year 5	5191	Year 10	8136

This effect arises because the amount that is charged is the gain computed according to CGT rules. Thus the gain in Year 1 is computed as follows:

	£
Sale Proceeds	12,000
Cost $12,000 \times \dfrac{100,000}{100,000\ +\ 12,000}$	10,715
Gain	1,285

National Savings

In recent years the government has placed a good deal of emphasis on keeping the rates of interest offered on the various National Savings investments competitive with their market rivals. It is now possible to obtain a worthwhile return and enjoy complete security of captial by investing in this way. In addition, National Savings are one of the few investments that pay interest without deduction of tax at source.

National Savings Income Bonds

Interest is paid on a monthly basis without deduction of tax. The interest rate is variable and subject to notice of change. You may cash part of your holding in multiples of £1,000, but you must keep a minimum of £2,000 invested. There are stringent penalties if you wish to redeem all or part of your capital at short notice which could mean forfeiting some or all of the interest.

National Savings Indexed Income Bond

Based on a term of ten years, the bond is designed to pay a high level of income which rises in line with inflation. The starting rate is 8 per cent per annum before tax and the income is paid out monthly. At the end of each year the sum is increased sufficiently to offset the rate of inflation over the previous years. The drawback is that while the income goes up, the capital value remains static so that no protection from inflation is offered in respect of the sum invested. Redemption terms are the same as those under the Income Bond.

National Savings Deposit Bond

This bond is designed to attract those who like an interest bearing investment which capitalises the interest rather than paying it as income. As with the Income Bond, interest is credited gross. Repayment is at three months' notice but there is an interest penalty if the investment is redeemed within one year of purchase.

National Savings Certificates (*Fixed interest variety*)

No interest is paid, but after a stated period, usually five years, the certificates can be redeemed at a higher value than the issue price. Certificates may be encashed with an increased value after one year, but the rate of interest is progressive and the full return can only be obtained by holding the certificates for the full term. The capital gain is free of all tax.

These certificates can also be used to produce an income. In effect this can be achieved by cashing a specified number of certificates each year to cream off the appreciation and at the end of the period the remaining certificates will repay the original investment. As the gain is tax free this can be an extremely tax efficient means of providing spendable income for the higher rate taxpayer.

Example

32nd Issue yielding 8.75% if held for 5 years:

Investment of £5,000.00 secures 200 certificates.

End of year	Certificates cashed	Income	Interest %
1	16	426.08	8.52
2	15	429.45	8.58
3	14	435.54	8.71
4	12	410.28	8.20
5	11	418.33	8.36

Remaining 132 certificates repay £5,019.96.

This exercise can be undertaken with most issues, and the number of certificates encashed is approximately the same in each case.

Index-Linked National Savings Certificates

Provided the certificates are held for more than a year the redemption value is equal to the original purchase price, increased in proportion to the increase in the Retail Prices Index which has occurred between the month of the purchase and the month of redemption. In addition to this index linking, holders can also receive a supplementary payment, and at the end of five years a further bonus is also payable on encashment. Once again, the capital gain is free of all taxes and the certificates guarantee to provide a return which beats inflation.

Insurance company schemes

Insurance companies have had income producing investments for many years. Where a regular level of income is required, an insurance company scheme could be useful. Unfortunately, they are a little complicated, but nevertheless they have proved popular for those who are prepared to tie up part of their capital for five to ten years.

These schemes comprise two separate parts:

(1) Temporary annuity (see p 229 for an explanation of an annuity)
(2) Endowment assurance policy for ten years.

Most of your capital investment is applied to purchase a temporary annuity providing a level income. The annuity payments may be made yearly (starting one year from the date you start your plan) or monthly (commencing one month after the starting date), and will be made directly to your bank account.

The balance of your capital investment is the first premium on the endowment assurance policy. The secondary subsequent premiums are met from the net annuity payments and will normally be paid by direct debiting mandate from your bank account.

The combination of annuity and bond will provide:

Income Any payments from the annuity not used to fund the regular premiums under the bond are available as net income.

Capital The proceeds of the endowment assurance policy at the end of the period are payable to you either as a tax free cash sum, or you may choose to take a tax free income from the proceeds.

There is no guarantee that the amount repaid by the insurance company at the end of the ten years will equal the original investment. This is dependent on current bonus levels remaining the same as they are when the money is invested and of course these may well reduce. Nevertheless, there is a degree of protection against this happening in that the scheme can be set up taking into account a lower bonus rate. In this case the income is lower but in the event of bonuses remaining at the level they are today there would be a capital gain at the end of ten years. This gain would be free of all tax.

It is of course important to understand that in order to obtain the full benefit from this type of plan it has to be maintained for the full ten years.

Annuities

The traditional investment for a retired person used to be a purchased life annuity. In its usual form you pay a lump sum to an insurance company, which then promises to pay you an income for however long you live.

What you get from an annuity depends on the following factors:

● interest rates generally available at the time you purchase the annuity,
● your age at the time you start the annuity,
● your sex.

If you are a man of, say, 65 when you buy your annuity you have a life expectancy of about 15 years (a definition of life expectancy is included in the *General Introduction* at the front of this book). The insurance company constructs the annuity to repay the capital to you over those 15 years and pay interest on the outstanding capital. The repayments (which therefore consist of partly repaid capital and interest) are calculated so that they are equal for the rest of your life, even if you live longer than 15 more years.

As a result, for any given purchase price, an annuity is higher for older people (and it will obviously be higher if interest rates at the time are high). On the other hand annuities for women are lower because all the available evidence shows that women live longer than men.

The interest 'element' is taxed at source but the tax can be reclaimed if you are a non taxpayer.

There is a wide variety of annuities and you can arrange to have the income paid every month, quarter, half year or year. You can also buy an annuity which will pay out a certain minimum amount, regardless of whether you survive. One arrangement which is particularly popular is the so called capital protected annuity. In this, the insurance company guarantees to return the purchase price of the annuity, either in a series of payments while you are alive, or by making up the difference by a lump sum when you die. A pension is a form of annuity and this is usually arranged on the basis of monthly payments with a guaranteed minimum of five years' income.

Annuity contracts cannot usually be cashed in once they have started. If they could, anyone who had bought one would endeavour to surrender it as soon as there was any sign of his health deteriorating. This the insurance company cannot allow since it depends on the profits which it makes from those who die early to pay for the losses which it makes on those who live longer than expected. It is this pooling of risk which makes the annuity so useful. It enables the insurance company to pay out a higher proportion of capital each year than would be prudent for an individual to select himself.

The main drawback with level payment annuities is, of course, the possibility of a return to high levels of inflation. Many people who bought annuities 20 years ago when they were 65 found that their income had lost two thirds of its purchasing power within little more than a decade.

The fact remains that annuities offer the highest possible continuing income. The older you are, the better will be the return and a 75 year old man could get more than £200 a year for an investment of £1,000. The time to use annuities is once a man is past 70 and a woman is over 75. Many insurance companies offer annuities which increase the amount paid out each year or two. These are generally uncompetitive since the tax free content does not rise and the initial return is greatly reduced in order to make possible the higher payouts later on.

Annuity home income schemes

It is undoubtedly true that many people invest considerable sums in their homes on the grounds that when they retire the property can be sold and part of the sale proceeds used as spending money. It is also true that many of these people eventually decide to stay in their home and consequently find their cash resources are lower than they would wish. For these people one answer to their problem is to use their home to provide spendable income and this can be done without suffering undue inconvenience. This can be achieved by arranging a home income scheme on the strength of the value that has been built up in the property. Essentially the scheme works like this:

(1)   The home owner takes a mortgage on the property up to £30,000 on an 'interest only' basis. Tax relief is gained on the interest provided that at least 90 per cent of the amount raised is used to buy an annuity.

(2)   The home owner purchases an annuity which is sufficient to cover the interest on the mortgage and leave enough over to use as spendable income.

(3)   When the home-owner (or owners where there is a couple) dies the house is sold and the mortgage is repaid — the sale proceeds, less the outstanding mortgage, form part of the deceased estate. Some protection can be obtaind to cover the position if the home owner dies within a short period after setting up the plan. For example, a slightly lower annuity may be payable on the basis that part of the loan will be repaid if the person dies within the first four years.

Certain conditions must be met before such a scheme can be arranged, and generally they are applicable only to the very elderly. In the case of a single person they normally have to be at least 70 years of age, and a married couple must have a combined age of 150.

As an example of the level of income that can be produced, a 75 year old woman arranging a £25,000 loan would receive spendable income of about £1,400 if she pays tax at the basic rate. The scheme can be adapted to those who wish to raise some capital as well as receive an income.

Provided you are in the right age bracket and you have a property worth more than £15,000 then you could consider such a scheme. It represents a useful way of using capital 'locked away' in your home and the use of a loan in this way reduces the value of your estate for inheritance tax purposes.

14 Equity and property investments

Until index-linked gilts were introduced, interest bearing investments provided no protection against inflation. Even now, the role which they can fill is limited and they certainly do not provide any mechanism by which you can share in the increasing wealth of the country. As a result, the basis of any long-term growth investment plan must be equities (ie stocks and shares) and/or property based. During the 1970s, many observers favoured putting the greater emphasis upon property. In the last few years, the pendulum has swung back to favouring equities. This seems to be largely a reaction to the way the different types of investment have performed.

In the five years up to the end of 1986, UK equities rose by approximately 200 per cent while a typical group of properties rose by something like 40 per cent. In the five years up to the beginning of 1978, the typical share portfolio with income reinvested showed a return of only 20 per cent over the whole period, while a typical group of properties increased by 30 per cent or more.

Whether you are investing in shares or property, you will need to follow similar principles. The most important rule is to diversify your investment. This simply means not putting all your eggs in one basket. Both types of investment carry risks, and it is unnecessarily foolhardy to leave yourself completely exposed to an isolated piece of bad luck. In 1960 few shares were more highly regarded than Rolls Royce yet this did not stop the company failing ten years later. There are many similar though less well known examples of property investments which proved equally unrewarding.

Less than 20 years ago, it was difficult for anyone except the very rich to acquire a diversified investment in a number of properties. The reason for this was simply their cost. If a person was going to buy even half a dozen properties, he had to restrict himself to comparatively small ones, and even then would have tied up several hundred thousand pounds in present day money. It is unlikely that he would want to do this, since many of the most attractive investment opportunities are in larger more expensive property.

In contrast, the medium-sized investor had no trouble in obtaining a diversified portfolio of ordinary shares. He could put either a few hundred or few thousand pounds into each of a dozen or so companies. Alternatively, he could purchase the shares of an investment trust which itself held shares in many different companies. If he took advantage of this method of spreading his risk, he had to deal with a complicating factor. This is that the shares of investment trusts, just like those of any other company dealt with on the Stock Exchange, fluctuate in accordance with supply and demand. The result if sentiment moved against the investment trust could be for its share price to fall even though the value of the underlying securities rose. Alternatively, if demand for the trust's shares increased, their price could rise even if the underlying assets declined.

The 1960s saw the rapid expansion of the unit trust movement. This made it possible for even the smallest investor to obtain a stake in a diversified and managed portfolio of ordinary shares.

Just as unit trusts were set up to provide a ready made diversified investment in shares, property companies were set up to do the same in their field. The situation was, however, rather different since the property companies were often managed in a much more entrepreneurial way than investment trusts. They were frequently highly geared and as a result made considerable development profits. Attractive as these investments were, they were hardly a substitute for a direct stake in bricks and mortar.

Equities

Ordinary shares, (or equities as they are sometimes called), are a company's risk capital; the investor who buys them expects a reasonable and rising level of dividend income and also a rise in the share price, but there is no certainty of either. If these expectations are fulfilled, then the investor is rewarded for taking the risk that the company might have encountered trading problems and that dividends might have fallen and the share price slumped. It is this risk which separates shares from other commonly held investments such as National Savings Certificates, building society shares and government stock. Where a person takes a risk with his capital he expects a higher than average return and historically this has proved to be the case.

In a recent study by stockbrokers Barclays de Zoete and Wedd it is revealed that shares have given a positive real return in 40 of the last 68 years. Allowing for the reinvestment of gross income there is no period of 20 years or more since 1919 in which equities have failed to give a positive real return. The average real return since 1919 has been 7 per cent per annum.

This long-term performance compares favourably with that of building society shares as the following table illustrates:

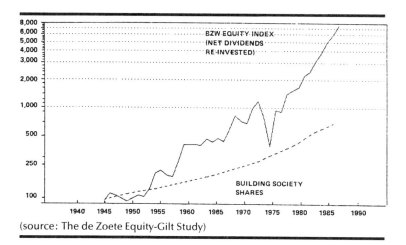

(source: The de Zoete Equity-Gilt Study)

Not only do shares provide capital growth, but they are also a long-term means of generating income. Dividends increased by 9 per cent in real terms in 1986, the fifth successive year of real share dividend increase.

While the table shows how well shares have performed in the long term, it also clearly demonstrates what can happen to share prices during periods of economic difficulties, as was experienced in the 1970s. As mentioned in previous chapters, personal circumstances will dictate whether a *direct* investment in shares is suitable for you, but if past experience is any guide, exposure to the stock market in some form should be seriously considered by most investors.

Your own portfolio

There is no reason at all why you cannot run a share portfolio yourself if you want to. Indeed, if you enjoy investment and are able to devote the time to it, then you may be lucky and do much better for yourself than you would by pooling your money with others and having it handled by professional investment managers. Despite this, investment is not an easy matter and is *extremely* time consuming if it is to be done properly. In addition, the pooled funds handled by professional managers do possess some important tax advantages and the stockbrokers' fees etc paid by the managers when changing investments are charged at a lower rate than that which applies to small investors' transactions. As a result an increasing number of people have chosen to use this route rather than handling their own portfolio.

Unit trusts

Unit trusts are designed to allow a large number of people to pool their money to buy shares. They permit existing investors to sell out and new ones to come in with no difficulty. The organisation of a unit trust is undertaken by a management company which is also responsible for choosing investments. The assets themselves are held by a trustee, who makes sure that the interests of the investors are taken care of. This structure has worked so well that there has never been a unit trust failure.

Example

Suppose a manager collects £1 million to start a trust. It is decided that the fund is to be invested in equal amounts in two companies, both of whose shares stand at £2.

    Investment in Company A: 250,000 shares @ £2
    Investment in Company B: 250,000 shares @ £2
    Total investment   £1,000,000

The investors between them now hold one million units @ £1 each—the precise number of units each has depends on how much they invested in the first place.

Suppose now at the next valuation, shares in company A are now £3 whereas shares in B are still £2. The total investment is now worth £1.25 million and each unit has increased in value to £1.25. If *new* investors wish to join the trust, this is the price (the offer price) at which they buy in. If existing investors wish to sell units, the manager agrees to buy them from them for a slightly lower price (the bid price). This price difference covers the costs of running the unit trust.

Types of fund

When unit trusts started there were only three types of fund recognised generally. These were income, general and growth funds, and corresponded to the main needs of different classes of investor. The objective of the growth fund is to seek to achieve the greatest possible capital appreciation. Managing an income fund is rather less straightforward. The object is to secure a high income for investors and some capital appreciation. It is a matter of priorities: a successful income trust will aim primarily to produce a steadily rising flow of distributions and will only be concerned with capital performance as a secondary consideration.

In a general trust, in contrast, both capital and income get equal weight. This means that the managers may accept a cut in income if this would seem likely to produce a more than commensurate improvement in the capital performance. On the other hand, they would certainly not totally disregard the interests of those who bought units in order to enjoy the distributions from them. If the income fell at one point, they would generally expect to restore it at the earliest opportunity.

Today, the situation has become much more complicated. There are now more than 1,000 different unit trusts divided into no fewer than 15 different categories.

See table overleaf

Sector index performance to 31 December 1986

Investment of £1000 at the beginning of the period

	1 year £	3 years £	5 years £
UK general	1188	1807	2904
UK growth	1239	1800	2871
UK equity income	1253	1983	3266
UK mixed income (pref/equity)	1195	1804	2952
North American	1049	1206	2087
Far Eastern	1567	1819	2457
Japan	1589	2079	3856
Australia	1347	1039	1236
Europe	1424	2587	4640
International	1244	1550	2563
Commodity & energy	1240	989	1315
Finance & property shares	1230	1851	2778
Investment trust units	1245	1722	3109
Gilt & fixed interest growth	1048	1219	1976
Gilt & fixed interest income	1031	1180	1774

(source: *Money Management*, February 1987)

The sector index performance figures beside each class of funds show the average performance of all the trusts in the group. They are calculated by reinvesting the net income after tax in the purchase of further units so as to permit an overall comparison of the different types of fund.

Interesting as past performance figures may be, it is important not to exaggerate their significance. What matters to you is their performance *in the future*, not what happened last week, last year or a decade ago. The most that the past can do is give a rough guide to the future and you must accept that you are unlikely to choose the best performing trust. Your aim should be to make certain that you don't get one of the worst. You won't go far wrong if you use one of the better established groups, since their performance is likely to prove sound over the medium to long term.

Tax treatment

Disposals of investments held in unit trusts are exempt from CGT so that the managers can switch their investments without being concerned about the tax liabilities. However, you as an investor may be liable for CGT when you sell units.

Income received by the unit trust is distributed in the form of dividends. These dividends are paid out net of tax at basic rate, but the tax withheld (29 per cent) can be reclaimed if you are not liable for the tax — for example if you are able to make a repayment claim because your personal allowance exceeds your state pension and any other untaxed income that you may have.

Investment bonds

These are lump sum investments issued by life assurance companies. They cover a broad range of investments and through them it is possible to invest in unit-linked funds invested in shares, properties, gilt-edged securities, interest-bearing investments and so on. There are also combined funds which invest in a range of different types of investment (typically a combination of property, shares and interest-bearing investments). These combined funds (or 'managed' funds as they are more commonly known) have been very popular since their introduction in the early 1970s.

The insurance company will specify the minimum initial investment which it will accept in a bond, and this is typically £1,000. Sometimes they will allow a smaller additional investment, but even then the amount is likely to be £500. The charges are similar to those levied by unit trusts, being usually a combination of an initial charge (the difference between the offer and bid price) levied when your money goes in and a recurring annual charge. Typically the initial charge is 5 per cent (plus a rounding amount) together with an annual management charge of 0.75 per cent per annum.

Although there is a minimum initial investment, you are normally free to make regular withdrawals from the fund even if this means that you fall below the minimum level. This is necessary because the bonds do not normally distribute the income which they earn but reinvest it within the fund. Many bonds allow you to specify how much you wish to withdraw at any one time although most of them fix a minimum withdrawal of £50. It is customary for the insurance companies to allow you to switch between one fund and another without charge or after payment of a nominal amount.

In structure, investment bonds are similar to unit trusts. They are 'pooled' investments and the individual investor's holding is represented by units which rise and fall in value in line with the value of the underlying investments. On the other hand, the tax treatment is completely different.

Tax on cashing in the bond

Gains realised on the disposal of bonds are not subject to CGT. They are, however, potentially liable to income tax.

A basic rate taxpayer who cashes in an investment bond will not normally have to pay tax on the gain. However, if you are a higher rate taxpayer, or if the gain when added to your other income lifts you into the higher tax brackets, then you will be liable to higher rate tax on the gain — but not basic rate tax.

For example, if you pay tax at a top rate of 40 per cent, then the gain will be taxed at 13 per cent (40 per cent–27 per cent). If you pay tax at a top rate of 45 per cent, the gain will be taxed at 18 per cent.

If the gain falls partly into the 40 per cent band and partly into the 45 per cent band, then a proportionate rate of between 40 and 45 per cent will be calculated and levied on the total gain, less the basic rate of 27 per cent. Furthermore, a special relief known as 'top slicing' relief (see p 118) may be available to reduce the tax payable — and by shrewd planning you may be able to time your disposal to avoid paying very much tax at all.

Partial cashing in

In the same way, if you cash in part of a bond you may be taxed at higher rates. Calculating the 'gain' in each case would be complex and so there is an agreed scheme — which offers, as a by product, the opportunity to draw a tax free 'income'.

(a) Each year, you may withdraw up to 5 per cent of the *original* value of your bond without incurring any tax liability at the time.

(b) You may do this for up to 20 years (or until the total equals 100 per cent if you withdraw less than 5 per cent a year).

(c) You may accumulate the 5 per cent allowances and then make a larger withdrawal, again without any tax liabilty at the time (eg you could withdraw nothing for ten years and then withdraw 50 per cent).

Every time you make a partial withdrawal, the total amounts withdrawn to-date are compared with the cumulative 5 per cent allowances. If, at any time you exceed your allowances, you will be liable for tax at higher rates on the excess and the accumulation starts all over again.

When you finally surrender the bond, the final proceeds and all the amounts you have withdrawn are added together and the overall gain is then liable to tax at the higher rates.

Therefore, bonds can pay a useful part in tax planning. You can withdraw an 'income' of 5 per cent with no liability to tax at the time. If you finally cash in the bond when you are likely to be paying lower rates of tax (eg in retirement) you may escape a tax liability altogether.

Types of fund

As with unit trusts, investment bonds offer the full range of funds to their investors. While most insurance companies tend to confine the choice to five or so general funds, some companies offer a far wider selection. In the main there is a choice of an equity fund (comprising mainly ordinary shares), a fixed interest fund (investing mainly in government stocks and other interest-bearing investments), an overseas fund (which concentrates on shares quoted on foreign stockmarkets), a property fund and a managed fund. Of this range, the last two are arguably the most important as they are to an extent unique to insurance bonds.

Property funds

If you want to invest in property through a UK fund you have to use an insurance bond since unit trusts are not allowed to invest directly in property.

Just as unit trusts are invested in the shares of companies, property bonds put their money into offices, factories and other buildings. The size of property bond funds varies very greatly, with the biggest worth over £500m and some of them only a few hundred thousand pounds. This difference in size is much more significant for property bonds than it is for equity funds. There are some advantages in running a small portfolio of ordinary shares. In contrast, a large property bond fund is considerably easier to manage than a small one.

Many of the best investment opportunities involve the purchase and development of large office blocks. These cost many millions of pounds and there is no way in which they can be afforded by the small fund. In addition, the large funds have invariably got that way by growing over many years. This means that the inflow of the new money is a comparatively small proportion of the total fund. Many small funds are new and in contrast their inflow of new money is frequently a high proportion of the fund.

It can take a long time to negotiate the purchase of a property and it is difficult to judge in advance how much a property fund will have to invest. As a result, if money flows in faster than expected, a small fund may find itself with almost as much of its assets in cash as in property. This may or may not produce a reasonable investment result but it is certainly not the object of investing in a property bond. Similar considerations apply to the possibility of investors liquidating their holdings. A small property fund may maintain a higher degree of liquidity because it has a much smaller selection of properties to sell if holdings are redeemed. The alternative is for the managers to defer the redemption of these holdings until sales are completed.

Managed funds

Managed funds have become extremely popular in recent years and virtually every significant unit-linked insurance company offers one. Their objective is to provide an even wider spread of investment by investing in property and fixed interest investments in addition to straightforward equity investments. The proportions of each type of investment in the fund vary according to the prevailing investment conditions of the time and the fund managers will alter the proportions as investment conditions change.

There are a variety of reasons for their popularity. Although shares have produced spectacular performance in the last few years, showing a rise of 200 per cent over five years, they are liable to violent fluctuation. Property is much more stable but has only shown an increase of about 40 per cent over the same period. Managed funds have succeeded in combining the two forms of investment and have produced a typical rise of just over 110 per cent. This combination of steadiness with performance is the answer for many investors. It is particularly important to avoid wide fluctuations when you may need to draw on your capital. This is the position of many retired people so that managed funds appeal particularly to them.

Flexibility

Investment bonds have certain features which make them very flexible. Firstly, there is a facility to 'switch' between one fund and another. For example, if you have seen your money appreciate rapidly in the equity fund and you believe it would be a good idea to capitalise on your good fortune then you can simply instruct the life assurance company to take your money out of the equity fund and put it into another fund, such as the property fund. Such a switch has no tax consequences and the company does not normally make more than a small charge for carrying out this transaction.

The switching facility means that you can vary your investment position with the added advantage that there are no income tax or capital gains tax problems as a result.

15 Investment strategy

The last two chapters were descriptive rather than prescriptive and explained the main features of various types of investments. We now turn to a much more difficult subject: formulating an investment policy and setting up a portfolio of different investments.

Your investment policy, or 'strategy' should be based on your personal circumstances. The right strategy for you may not be appropriate for someone else. Before we go into this, ask yourself the following questions:

- What spendable income do you need *now*?
- What provision do you think you should make against inflation?
- How would your wife stand for income if you were to die in five, or ten, or fifteen years' time?
- What rate of tax applies to your investment income?
- Is this likely to change significantly in the future?
- How much of your capital do you need to keep readily available?
- Can you set aside *some* of your capital and invest this for the medium term so as to secure a better return?

To some extent you need to strike a balance between various considerations. You certainly do need to have ready access to some of your capital in case of an emergency but it is probably wasteful for you to invest all your capital in (say) a building society or high interest bank account. It is wasteful since:

(a)   it may be 'inefficient' from a tax point of view in that you may be paying more tax than you need,
(b)   the value of your capital will not increase, and

(c)   your real income will at best be static and may actually fall
      — when you take account of inflation.

Older people tend to be conservative investors — and rightly
so, but there is really no such thing as a 'riskless' investment. A
building society or bank account *seems* to be risk free since
you can always withdraw £100 for every £100 that you put in.
However, it carries a hidden risk that the capital value may be
eroded and the interest paid out may fall if interest rates go
down in the future. So an apparently risk free investment may
actually leave you exposed twice over — the level of your interest income may go down at a time when you need more
income to take care of inflation.

By contrast, asset backed investments such as insurance bonds
and unit trusts are certainly not risk free investments, the value
of your units may go down as well as up — especially in the
short term. But in some respects these broadly based asset
backed investments may seem a better bet in the long run.

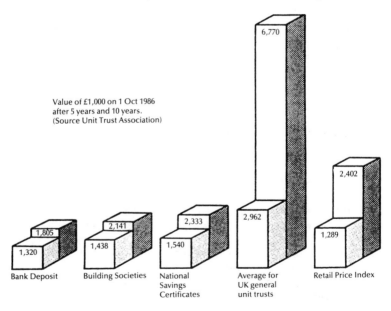

Value of £1,000 on 1 Oct 1986
after 5 years and 10 years.
(Source Unit Trust Association)

6,770

2,402

2,962

2,333

2,141

1,805

1,540

1,438

1,320

1,289

Bank Deposit   Building Societies   National   Average for   Retail Price Index
                                      Savings   UK general
                                      Certificates   unit trusts

The point we are making is *not* that you should necessarily
invest most of your money in shares or unit trusts. This may or

may not be appropriate according to your personal circumstances, your views on the economy etc. What we are saying is that you should ask yourself who was really the more cautious investor — the person who kept all his money in a building society or a person who accepted a lower level of income on some of his capital because he expected the income to rise?

Some general principles

We believe that by applying the following ground rules you will avoid most of the pitfalls:

(1)   There must be ready access to some capital.
(2)   Any portfolio that is established with the primary objective of producing spendable income should be arranged in such a way as to produce a regular cash flow. Few retired people will wish to receive their income on an annual or half yearly basis. Income should be as regular as is practicable, and the choice of investments should be made with this requirement in mind.
(3)   Equity and property based investments should also play some part.
(4)   Undue risk should be avoided as far as possible — including the possibility of a serious reduction in interest rates.
(5)   Such investments need to be *managed* and unit-linked insurance funds and unit trusts are especially appropriate for the smaller investor.
(6)   Consistently good performance is the most important thing to look for when choosing a unit trust or insurance group.
(7)   Tax needs to be borne in mind. Insurance bonds may be an especially attractive way for a higher rate tax payer to invest. Also bear in mind investments which provide a tax free return such as National Savings Certificates.
(8)   Bear in mind the fact that tax free spendable 'income' can often be produced by taking capital gains on shares or unit trusts within the annual CGT exemption. Looked at in practical terms. £50,000 growing at 10 per cent per annum could produce £5,000 net 'income' from capital gains whereas a 60 per cent taxpayer would need to have £125,000 on deposit at 10 per cent in order to have £5,000 spendable income after tax.

Much of this should now be self-evident but it is worth dwelling on certain aspects.

Investments should be managed

There is no reason why you should not manage your own investments — if you have the time, expertise and inclination. However, investment can be a complex matter and most people delegate this work to a specialist.

Investments need to be monitored — especially stocks and shares. Someone needs to make sure that dividends are collected, rights issues taken up and so on. Even more importantly, someone needs to review the position from time to time to consider whether (for example) the time is now right to sell shares in Marks & Spencer, Hanson Trust or Guinness and to buy shares in British Gas, or to switch into gilts instead. If you invest via a fund all this is done for you.

Some investments are automatically managed to a high degree — for example insurance bond 'managed' funds. These may therefore particularly appeal to older investors who do not want to be worried by such matters and would rather rely upon a professional manager — so long as the cash register rings up at regular intervals!

Unit trusts are also managed in that you delegate to the fund managers decisions such as when to sell J Sainsbury shares and buy another stock. However, it has to be said that unit trusts are less broadly based than insurance company managed funds. Therefore you should spread your investment in unit trusts across several different trusts and take advice from time to time on whether you should switch funds. Unit trusts also reduce risk — your investment is spread over a number of different stocks and shares so the value of your investment is not as subject to fluctuation as if you invested directly in one or two companies.

Invest in unit trusts for income

Although capital values fluctuate, the dividends tend to be more stable and to follow a gradually rising trend. If you need to provide income for a long period it may well be advisable to invest in a range of unit trusts for an income which is not guaranteed but is likely to increase steadily.

The Unit Trust Association has published statistics comparing the income payable on an investment of £1,000 in a typical unit trust invested in UK equity shares, and the interest payable on a £1,000 building society deposit.

	Building society £	Unit trust £
Over five years		
Initial net income	93	74
Position at 1 October 1986	66	100
Over ten years		
Initial net income	74	70
Position at 1 October 1986	66	148
Over fifteen years		
Initial net income	49	33
Position at 1 October 1986	66	135

This pattern is borne out by statistics covering the past ten years. The dividend yield on ordinary shares has consistently increased even though there have been periods when the capital value has fallen.

Consistency counts

There is a very wide variation in the performance of insurance bond funds and unit trusts. However, some groups do consistently perform better than average.

In our view, it is consistency which is most important. Statistically it is unlikely that the fund which performed best over the past 12 months will be next year's winner. Almost every group has one or two funds which have performed well but you will be lucky to pick next year's best performing fund out of the 1,500 bond funds and unit trusts. You are much more likely to do well if you look for groups with all round performance which shows in their funds consistently performing better than average — ideally with most of the group's funds being in the top 25 per cent for their sector.

Relevant questions to ask yourself are:

● Is the company a member of the Life Offices Association and/or the Unit Trust Association?

- Is it a large group with substantial research facilities and efficient administration?
- Has the ownership of the group recently changed? (This could indicate some changes in the personnel involved in managing investments etc)
- How well does the group appear in statistics produced by specialist magazines such as *Money Management* or *Planned Savings*? Don't just look at one year in isolation — what has the performance been like over one year, three years and five years?

Tax and your investments

It is not just those who are subject to higher rate tax who need to consider this aspect. You may, for example, be caught by the age allowance 'trap'.

As we have seen (p 118) you may be entitled to an increased personal allowance once you (or your wife) have attained the age of 65.

The basic single person's allowance is increased to £2,960 and the married person's allowance is increased to £4,675. However, the increased allowance is available only if your total taxable income is below £9,800. If it goes over that limit you lose £2 of the extra allowance for every £3 of extra income. So you pay twice: 27 per cent tax on the excess income *plus* 27 per cent on the amount of the allowance lost — in practice it is the same as paying tax at 44 per cent on the top 'slice' of your income.

What can be done about this? Consider investing some capital in insurance bonds. You may actually be able to increase your net spendable income.

Example

Let us take a typical case where a person has income of £10,600 and assume that the capital is earning income of 6% per annum. If the person were to invest £20,000 in an insurance bond he might reduce his taxable income to below £9,800 but increase his spendable income by taking the tax free 5% withdrawals each year.

	'Before'	'After'
	£	£
Income	10,600	9,400
Less married age allowance	4,142	4,675
Taxable income	6,458	4,725
Tax thereon	1,743	1,276
Income	10,600	9,400
Add 5% withdrawal from insurance bond		1,000
	10,600	10,400
Less tax	1,743	1,276
Spendable income	£8,857	£9,124

Bonds are also a very attractive way for higher rate tax payers to invest. If you would otherwise pay tax at 60 per cent the value of the 5 per cent tax free withdrawals is equivalent to taxable income of 12.5 per cent.

Another thing that can be said in favour of bonds is that no CGT liability arises when you switch investment 'internally' by moving out of (say) the equity fund into the international or property fund.

Taxation is obviously a complicated area and you need to take advice on the tax implications when structuring your portfolio and also when changing investments. Bonds are a way of avoiding these problems.

Putting these principles into practice

It's impossible to say how much should go into any particular type of investment, as each portfolio will be arranged to suit individual circumstances. However, most people will not want to immediately lock all their money up in long-term investments, but rather will take the view that part should be kept for short-term use, some may be needed after five years, and the balance can be salted away for long-term investment. By adopting this approach, certain categories of investment wil automatically select themselves.

Within three years
This is the cash you just feel you might need in the next couple of years. Some will need to be available immediately — the remainder can be on longer-term deposit to obtain a higher return.

How much money do you feel should be immediately accessible? £500? £1,000? Whatever amount you feel is right should go into your building society, or into one of the interest bearing current accounts, which allows withdrawals without notice.

How much more do you feel comfortable about being available at, say three months' notice? Perhaps you would feel easier in your mind if you were able to fund holidays and contingencies (eg a major repair to the car) over the next two or three years. That's the amount that should go into a building society offering the best rates you can find, which will normally entail having to give notice.

What this will provide is a cushion against unexpected emergencies, and a cushion against adverse investment conditions elsewhere. It will also enable you to plan your other investments without worrying about whether you will have the money. On the other side of the coin, a float will provide the means to take an unexpected investment opportunity. You will also get a high level of income.

Three to five years
This is the money you will feel happier about if you know it's going to be back in your hands within five years. As this is still a relatively short period you should put the money required during this period into gilts and National Savings.

Gilts: Even though, at the time of writing, real interest rates are historically high, there is the possibility that over the medium term these will fall. High coupon gilts offer a flexible means of guaranteeing a fixed income for a pre-determined period. If interest rates do fall, it may be possible to sell the stock and make a tax free capital gain.

For those who do not need income, there is a choice of gilts that will produce guaranteed capital growth. These are the low coupon stocks, which stand at a price below the redemption value; or the index-linked stocks where the value is increased in line with inflation. Both are useful vehicles for providing a safe and risk free home for short-term capital.

National Savings Certificates: The tax exempt nature of this investment, and the competitive returns they offer, make them particularly attractive to the higher rate taxpayer. Like gilts, they can be purchased on the basis of a fixed return, or an index-linked basis.

As explained earlier, National Savings Certificates can be used to provide the investor with capital growth or income.

More than five years

This is where equities, and equity-based investments such as unit trusts and/or investment bonds come into the reckoning (indeed they are longer-term investments and you shouldn't be looking at them as shorter-term investments). Invest for income if that's what you need, but look forward to capital growth over the long term as well.

It is perfectly possible to construct a portfolio of unit trusts specifically designed to provide you with an income. Unit trusts make income payments every six months, six unit trusts packaged together can therefore provide a monthly income. These 'monthly income plans' are marketed by the major companies and are increasingly used to supplement income in retirement.

The capital value of the investment will fluctuate (one only has to look back to 1974) but the overall level of dividend income from a widely spread portfolio of shares (which is what a unit trust is) has remained remarkably steady over the years.

Unit trusts have tended to be looked at as purely capital investments. They are not — they are being used more and more to provide income with the very real prospect of capital growth over the longer term as well.

Used as a vehicle to provide income and capital growth, the

managed bond can also play a useful and rewarding role. This is especially true where the investor is a higher rate taxpayer at the time the bond is established, but his rate of tax is reduced to the basic rate when the bond is encashed.

A judicious combination of these investments should fulfil all the criteria laid down in our investment policy. As a result, your investment returns should be good and much of the concern that is associated with investment should be eliminated. You will, of course, need to review the position regularly, to ensure that you are obtaining the best possible returns.

16 Retiring on a low income

Inevitably there will be people who make only very limited provision, or perhaps no provision at all, for their old age. Consequently money will be extremely tight and it may be necessary to seek assistance simply to make ends meet. While this assistance will always be of a limited amount, it will at least ensure that the basic necessities of life are provided.

This section deals with the following questions:

●   What will you get in extra help from the state?
●   Who is eligible for additional state benefits?
●   What other sources are there for advice and assistance?

Supplementary pension

Unlike other state pension, supplementary pension is not available as of right, but is provided on a means tested basis. Therefore, what you get, if anything at all, will depend on your income at the time you claim. The object of supplementary pension is to ensure that you have a minimum sum on which to live after paying for the mortgage (or rent) and rates. In practical terms, supplementary pension will top up your income so that it does not fall far short of the full basic retirement pension plus the cost of paying mortgage interest (or rent) and rates.

Any supplementary pension payable to you will of course be reduced if you are in receipt of an occupational or personal pension, or if you have part-time earnings above a certain amount.

In addition to the pension, you may also be able to claim extra benefit for heating costs, and the amount you will receive will depend upon family circumstances. At best this will, however, amount to £5 or so a week.

If you do qualify for supplementary pension then you may also be able to obtain a lump sum payment for some one-off expenses. This can cover such things as the cost of moving, the purchase of furniture and household equipment and house repairs.

Finally, you will not qualify for supplementary pension if you have savings of £3,000 or more. This can take the form of building society or bank deposits, National Savings Certificates, Premium Bond or other investments. However, it does not include a car, any items of valuable furniture or jewellery.

If you believe that you can claim, then complete the blue page at the back of the retirement pension book or use the claim form in leaflet SB 1. Alternatively, call at your local DHSS office and discuss the matter with an official. There is also a free DHSS telephone advice service. You simply dial 100 and ask for Freefone DHSS.

Other help

You can get free prescriptions if you are over pension age irrespective of your income. For those on supplementary pension or a low income there is also free dental treatment, dentures and glasses.

Going into hospital

The older you get the more likely it is that you will spend some time in hospital. Bear in mind that your pension will be reduced if you go into hospital for in-patient treatment on the NHS. This will happen after eight weeks or immediately if you are living in a local authority home or similar place before going into hospital. Currently the reduction is £7.15 if you have a dependant and £14.30 if you don't.

Local authorities and other organisations

If you are not able to obtain supplementary pension, then the next step is to approach the local council for housing benefit. Like supplementary pension, this is means tested and what you will get will depend on your other income. The local authority will provide a form which when completed will be vetted in order to determine how much, if anything, you can get. Provided your income is not significantly above the supplementary pension level then you stand a good chance of obtaining some additional assistance.

Other organisations may also be able to help if you are in financial difficulties. Each will need to be contacted separately. The Citizens Advice Bureaux may be able to help. Contact your local office — they are always a useful starting point and are able to offer advice on financial matters. Few charities provide direct assistance to elderly people who are in need of financial help. Nevertheless, organisations such as Age Concern and Help The Aged can give advice. The Royal United Kingdom Beneficent Association grant annuities to certain elderly persons who are impoverished or infirm. So do the Universal Beneficent Society but in this case you must be referred either by the Social Services or the DHSS. You could also contact the Distressed Gentlefolk's Aid Association whose activities include the provision of emergency grants.

A capital idea

If you own your own home it may be possible to raise some capital to carry out home improvements, without incurring the burden of loan repayments. A number of building societies are prepared to advance money on the security of a charge over the house. This is what normally happens when an ordinary mortgage is arranged. The difference is that there is no requirement to repay any of the capital that has been borrowed, this is reclaimed by the building society only when the house (or flat) is eventually sold. What you have to pay out is only the interest, and as a recipient of supplementary pension this cost is borne by the DHSS (see above).

The mortgage can be used to carry out much needed home improvements which will enhance the comfort of your retirement. Enquiries should be made at the nearest DHSS office.

Addresses

Citizens Advice Bureau — see local directory

Age Concern, 60 Pitcairn Road, Mitcham, Surrey, CR4 3LL

Help the Aged, 16–18 St James's Walk, London, EC1R 0BE

Royal United Kingdom Beneficent Association
6 Avonmore Road, London, W14 8RL

Universal Beneficent Society, 6 Avonmore Road,
London, W14 8RL

Distressed Gentlefolk's Aid Association, Vicarage Gate House,
Vicarage Gate, London, W8 4AQ.

Some leaflets you may find helpful

Available from any DHSS office

Subject	Reference number
Which benefit (a short summary of all the social security benefits)	FB 2
Retiring (your pension and other benefits)	FB 6
Your retirement pension	NP 32
Your retirement pension if you are widowed or divorced	NP 32A
Retirement benefits for married women	NP 32B
Earning extra pension by cancelling your retirement	NI 92
Retirement pension and widow's benefits payment direct into bank or building society account	NI 105
Non-contributory retirement pension for people over 80	NI 184
Christmas bonus: paid with some social security benefits	NI 229
Cash help: you can claim supplementary benefit	SB 1
Supplementary benefit: lump sum payments for special needs	SB 16
Help with heating costs for people getting supplementary benefit	SB 17
Supplementary benefit: the capital rule	SB 18
Supplementary benefit: weekly payments for special needs	SB 19
NHS dental treatment	D 11
NHS glasses	G 11
Fares to hospital	H 11
NHS prescriptions	P 11
Who pays less rent and rates	RR 1
Help for handicapped people	HB 1
Going into hospital	NI 9
Social security benefit rates and earnings rules	NI 196

17 Making a Will

There are few actions which give greater benefit for less cost than the making of a Will. Despite this, many people die without making one (ie they die intestate). The result with even the smallest estate is to cause confusion over who should obtain Letters of Administration in order to administer it. There are also likely to be complications if the estate has to be divided under the intestacy rules. Those with substantial assets may end up paying quite unnecessary inheritance tax (IHT) and, of course, it may well be that their estate is distributed in a way they do not approve of.

Intestacy

The law in Scotland is different, but in England and Wales, if you die without making a Will the intestacy rules will apply in the following way:

If you leave a widow but no children

All your personal chattels (ie furniture, paintings, car etc) will go to your surviving spouse, who will also be entitled to the first £85,000 of the rest of your property. He or she will have a half share in the remainder of the estate. If your parents are alive they will be entitled to the rest but otherwise the half share will go to any brothers or sisters you may have or to their children.

If you leave a widow and surviving children

Your spouse is still entitled to all your personal chattels, but he or she only gets the first £40,000. He or she then gets a life interest in one half of the remaining assets. The remainder goes to your children, who also receive the first half share when your spouse dies.

If you do not leave a widow but you leave children or grandchildren

If there is no spouse, but you leave children, the estate is divided equally between them. If one of your children has died before you, his children normally take the amount to which he would have been entitled.

If you do not leave a widow or children

When there are neither children nor a surviving spouse, the estate passes to the parents if they are alive. If they are not, the estate passes to any brothers and sisters, and then on to their children. If this does not produce an heir, the estate will pass to any surviving grandparents, or failing this will go to any aunts or uncles. If this fails to find an heir, the property will pass to the Crown. It is significant that common law wives and husbands obtain no benefit under the intestacy rules although they can apply to the court for 'reasonable provision'.

It is highly improbable that these rules will distribute your possessions in that way that you wish. Even if they will, dying intestate imposes extra burdens on your family which can be easily avoided. It is possible to make a Will yourself and there are a number of 'do-it-yourself' kits available. On the other hand, the charges that a solicitor will make are comparatively small, so that it normally makes sense to have professional advice.

The formalities

For a Will to be valid under English law, it must be signed in front of two witnesses who must sign the document themselves. Each witness should observe the other's signature as well as that of the testator. On the other hand, the witnesses are only there to witness the signature. There is no need for them to know the contents of the Will. A blind person cannot witness a Will, nor can somebody who is mentally ill. Otherwise, anyone can be a witness, although it should normally be someone over 18.

If you make your Will yourself, you want to be careful to choose witnesses who will not benefit under it. Any gift made to a witness, or the husband or wife of a witness, will be invalid, although this will not affect the rest of the Will. Any amendments or additions to the Will, which may be handwritten, should be signed by the testator and both witnesses in exactly the same way as the complete Will.

Choosing executors

One of the most important points about a Will is choosing the right executors to carry it out. The more complex your affairs, and the more elaborate your Will, the more important this is. Unfortunately, there is no straightforward answer. On the one hand, there are the executor and trustee services offered by the banks and one or two insurance companies. On the other, there is the possibility of appointing a member of the family, and in between the two lies the employment of a solicitor.

If you use a bank, you can be assured that the estate will be administered disinterestedly, and that the technical resources will be available to deal with any complexities which may arise. However the bank might charge £4,500 as executor for an estate worth £100,000. In contrast, a member of the family may well perform the same function for nothing.

The trouble is that Wills frequently lead to considerable ill feeling among families, and this can be greatly accentuated if the executor is himself interested, even if only indirectly. There is also the problem of finding a family member who is properly qualified to carry out the work involved if it is at all complicated. A solicitor will almost certainly charge less than a bank but the amount will vary according to the firm chosen. A small firm in the provinces is almost bound to charge less than a large London one, and will often give just as good a service. In either case, you will have the advantage of impartial administration. If you know the firm well, you can also expect a more personal service than that given by a bank.

The most common solution to these problems is to appoint more than one executor. This means that you choose a solicitor, or bank or insurance company and one or two friends or members of the family. The first one can provide the technical knowledge and do the work, while the others can supply a sense of urgency and a personal interest in the case.

Although it is important that Wills should be renewed, they are often left alone for many years. This can mean that when you die, your executors are no longer capable of administering your estate effectively. There is little point in appointing an executor who is the same age or older than you are.

The importance of flexibility

It is often possible to secure considerable tax savings by writing your Will so as to take fullest advantage of the reliefs available to you. The problem is that both the tax law and the size of your estate will change. This means that you should regularly review your Will at least once a year so as to make sure that it has not become outmoded. This is clearly impractical and fortunately there is a better and less time consuming method. This is to leave your executors the discretion to override the dispositions you have made. They can then change the conditions of your Will so as to avoid unnecessary taxation and also to take account of any other changes in conditions which you did not foresee.

This means giving your executors the right to decide how your estate will be distributed. There are however, a number of safeguards which ensure that this is strictly limited. Usually the Will will be in two parts. The first is quite conventional and disposes of the whole of the estate. It may well give a greater proportion of the assets to the surviving spouse than is likely to be necessary. These provisions will apply unless the executors decide to apply their discretion in the two years after the death. The second part of the Will sets out the executors' powers to override the main section. It sets out those beneficiaries to whom they can decide to distribute part of the estate. If a husband is concerned that too much may be given to other beneficiaries, he can make his widow one of the executors with a power of veto on any distributions. The same can of course be done by a wife who is concerned about her husband.

It is difficult to know how to divide your assets unless you know when you are going to die. If a man leaves a widow in her early sixties, he will probably want to leave her a considerable sum. She will need a house, and a sufficient income to maintain her independence. At the same time, she will want some reserves to guard her against inflation or other economic reverses over the next 20 or 30 years. There is no point in doing this for a widow in her eighties who is already in poor health.

In this case, there is every advantage in passing as many assets as possible over to a younger generation once the widow's needs have been taken care of. At the very least, it will often make sense to take advantage of the nil rate band, ie the maximum amount which can be left your children without any IHT being payable.

When assets are passed over, the beneficiaries may request that these should be given to their own children. This will give rise to income which is taxable only at the rate appropriate to them, rather than being aggregated with that of their parents.

A particular advantage of this arrangement is that the executors can have up to two years to decide whether or not to exercise their powers. Any action they take is backdated to the date of death, and taxation is assessed on that basis. This can be valuable since it means that the executors are able to act on the basis of knowledge which the testator could not possibly have possessed, enabling the Will to take account of both economic changes and altered circumstances within the family. Of course, IHT is due to be paid at the normal times, so interest may have to be paid if the exercising of the executors' discretion creates a liability which is settled late. This could well be the case when the whole of the estate has been left to the widow and it is decided to reduce the future IHT bill which would have to be paid when she died, by using some of the lower rates of tax on the husband's estate.

If this type of will is contemplated it is essential that it is drawn up by a solicitor.

The alternative

If a Will has not been written on a discretionary basis, a similar effect can be achieved as a last resort if those who benefit under it agree to vary its provisions.

A 'Deed of Variation' (sometimes called a 'Deed of Family Arrangement') made within two years will enable a person to transfer assets with no personal IHT or CGT implications. Hence, it permits post-death planning to be made by the beneficiaries, even if the deceased did not provide for it. On the other hand, it is normally more cumbersome and less efficient for income tax purposes than arranging the matter through a discretionary Will.

It is sometimes also possible to vary a Will by a beneficiary disclaiming a legacy. However, a disclaimer simply means that you give up your entitlement. You cannot direct that the property you have given up should fall to a particular person. The consequences will depend upon the other provisions of the Will.

Summary

If you do not make a Will, your assets will be disposed of according to the intestacy rules. Even if this broadly meets your intentions, the process is tiresome. There is, therefore, every reason to make a Will.

One of the most important points is the choice of the right executor or executors. There is much to be said for combining one or more members of the family with a disinterested person or organisation if the estate is complex. When it comes to writing a Will, there are strong arguments in favour of making it discretionary since there may be a long period between the writing of the Will and the time when it takes effect. If the Will is not discretionary, and turns out to be inefficient for tax purposes, much can be done by post-death Deeds of Variation or disclaimers.

Once you have made your Will, lodge it with your lawyer or bank and file a copy with your personal papers, together with a note saying where the original has been placed. It is also worth appending a schedule to both copies giving details of your bank accounts, solicitors, accountant, stockbroker, life insurance policies, building society accounts, savings certificates, shares, property owned at home and abroad and any other information that will enable your executors to handle matters promptly for the beneficiaries. Allied Dunbar have a free booklet called *Arranging Your Affairs* which includes a questionnaire which will provide the required information for your executors.

Finally don't hide away the odd million in a numbered Swiss bank account without giving anybody the details. It has happened!

18 Passing on your wealth

In this chapter we seek to deal with the following questions:

- How is Inheritance Tax (IHT) charged on death?
- How are lifetime gifts treated?
- What can be done to mitigate IHT?

Inevitably some of what follows will seem complicated and obscure—our tax system is like that. But it is worth persevering: Inheritance tax can be a heavy burden for the family of a person who ignores it altogether but it is often an *avoidable* tax. What is more, in many cases it is possible for a person to take preventive action without affecting his financial independence.

How is IHT charged on death?

When a person dies, his property at the date of death and any trust property in which he has a life interest (his 'estate') is said to 'pass', ie there is a capital transfer of the value of the property. Inheritance tax is charged on this transfer. The tax is charged at rates which rise progressively to a maximum rate of 60 per cent.

£	%	Tax on band £	Cumulative tax on upper figure £
0–90,000	nil		
90–140,000	30	15,000	15,000
140–220,000	40	32,000	47,000
220–330,000	50	55,000	102,000
over 330,000	60		

Bear in mind that lifetime gifts within seven years of death may have to be taken into account in order to fix the rate of tax payable on death. So that, if you die leaving property worth £246,000 but you made chargeable transfers of £90,000 (for example) during the past seven years, then the IHT payable will be computed thus:

Lifetime transfers	90,000		
Estate on death	240,000		
	£330,000		
IHT on cumulative transfers of £330,000		=	102,000
Less IHT on £90,000		=	nil
IHT payable on death			£102,000

£330,000 may sound an awful lot of money, but is it? Remember that there is no special relief for your home so you can have an estate which is subject to the maximum rate if you own a house worth £150,000 and have investments of £180,000.

Go through the following steps to work out the tax which might be payable upon your death:

Property owned by you	
Trust property where you have a life interest	
	————
Less property passing to your spouse	
	————
Add gifts made within the last seven years	
	————
Amount on which IHT is charged	
	————

In some cases you will find that you are going to leave more to the taxman than to your own family.

On the other hand, don't be too gloomy. After all, there are

various exemptions such as the exemption for property passing to your spouse and the charity exemption. Furthermore,
special reliefs may be available to reduce the value of certain
types of unquoted shares or business property owned by you.

Main exemptions

Transfers to your spouse

These are totally exempt except for the rather unusual situation
where the donor is domiciled in the UK but the donee is not. In
that case, the exemption is limited to £55,000.

This is clearly a very important exemption as it means that no
IHT will be payable on property which you leave your wife.

Gifts to charities

All gifts to registered charities are exempt whether they are
made during lifetime or on death.

Gifts for national purposes

Gifts to certain national bodies are totally exempt. These
include the National Gallery, the British Museum or any similar
national institution, any museum or art gallery in the UK which
is maintained by a local authority or university, the National
Trust, any university or university college in the UK and any
local authority or Government department.

Special reliefs

Business property relief

A 50 per cent deduction is allowed for the value of the following property:

●   a sole trader's business,
●   a partner's interest in his firm,
●   a controlling shareholding in a trading company.

The 1987 Budget also extended the 50 per cent deduction to
minority shareholdings in unquoted companies where the
holding exceeds 25 per cent of the company's ordinary share
capital.

A 30 per cent deduction is allowed from:

- property owned by a partner but used by his firm for its business,
- property owned by a controlling shareholder and used by his company for business purposes,
- smaller minority shareholdings in unquoted trading companies.

It is normally necessary for the property to have been held for at least two years in order to qualify.

Agricultural property relief

A 50 per cent deduction is allowed from the value of land where:

- the owner occupied it,
- a firm in which he was a partner occupied it,
- the owner was entitled to obtain vacant possession within twelve months.

A 30 per cent deduction is allowed from the value of other tenanted farmland.

Agricultural relief is only available for land situated in the UK, Channel Islands or Isle of Man. The land normally has to have been owned for two years if it is occupied or seven years if it is tenanted.

How are lifetime gifts treated?

Inheritance tax replaced capital transfer tax (CTT) in 1986. Capital transfer tax applied to virtually all lifetime gifts as well as to property passing on death (subject to specific exemptions for certain types of gifts). The main difference between IHT and CTT is that no tax is payable during lifetimes on property given away *provided*:

(a) the donor survives seven years; *and*
(b) the gift is an outright gift by an individual to another individual and not a transfer into a trust; *or*
(c) the gift is a transfer into a special type of trust for children aged below 25 called an 'accumulation and maintenance trust' or to a trust for disabled persons.

(*d*) the gift is a transfer to a trust where a beneficiary has an interest in possession.

Gifts which are exempt provided that the donor lives seven years are said to be 'potentially exempt transfers'. We deal with exempt gifts which are ignored even if you die within the seven year period on p 195.

If you die within the seven year period

The first consequence of dying within the seven years is that any potentially exempt transfers prove not to be exempt after all. Inheritance tax is payable at a proportion of the rates in force at the time of death, the proportion being determined by 'tapering relief'. However, although the tax rates used are those in force at the date of death, the tax is charged on the original value of the gift. Another peculiarity is that when fixing the rate applicable to the gift it is necessary to take account of chargeable transfers made during the seven years preceding the gift.

Example

A gave B on 1 May 1986 100 shares in an investment company ABC Ltd. The shares had a market value of £80,000. On 27 April 1993 A died. The shares in ABC Ltd were then worth £250,000.

The gift of £80,000 (*not* £250,000) becomes chargeable and tax would be chargeable at the rates in force at 27 April 1993. However, the IHT would take account of chargeable transfers made by A during the period 1 May 1979–1986 so that if A had made chargeable transfers during that period of £120,000 the IHT on the May 1986 gift would be calculated as follows:

value of gift	£ 80,000	
transfers made in preceding seven years	£120,000	
	£200,000	IHT thereon = £39,000
	deduct IHT on £120,000	= £ 9,000
IHT on £110,000 gift before 'tapering relief'		= £30,000

Tapering relief
Where an individual dies within seven years of making a potentially exempt transfer (PET) a proportion of the full tax is payable as follows:

Death in years	%
1–3	100
3–4	80
4–5	60
5–6	40
6–7	20

As A made the gift on 1 May 1986 but died on 27 April 1993, he died within seven years of the gift being made. As he died in year seven, only 20% of the IHT is payable ie 20% of £30,000 = £6,000 payable.

If A died possessed of property worth £140,000 the IHT on that property would be computed as follows:

Property passing on death	£140,000		
Gifts made in preceding seven years	£ 80,000		
	£220,000	IHT thereon =	£47,000
Less IHT payable on chargeable transfers of £80,000		=	–
IHT payable on death			£47,000

Actually the IHT would be charged at the rates in force at the date of death — we have simply used the rates presently in force for illustration.

Reservation of benefit

Until recently it was possible to 'give away your cake *and* eat it', ie make a gift of property which was effective for CTT purposes without giving up the income. Insurance companies produced standard arrangements intended to achieve just this ('inheritance trusts'). The replacement of CTT by IHT put an end to this and the Finance Act 1986 contains anti-avoidance provisions.

Basically, the rule is now that a gift is not effective for IHT purposes unless the donor is excluded from all benefit. If he actually enjoys some benefit, or if the gift is made in such a way that a benefit may be provided (for example, a gift is made into a discretionary trust under which the donor *could* benefit) he is said to have 'reserved benefit'. If he dies without giving up the reservation of benefit the value of the property at the date of death is included in his estate for IHT purposes. If the benefit is given up during his lifetime then he must survive a further seven years in order to avoid paying any tax.

Transfers which are exempt even if you don't survive seven years

Normal expenditure of income: There is also an exemption for gifts made out of income which are normal (ie habitual) expenditure and which do not reduce the donor's standard of living. This exemption usually covers gifts made by Deed of Covenant or premiums paid out of income or an insurance policy.

£250 exemption: There is an exemption for gifts not exceeding £250 for any one recipient in a tax year. The exemption is not available to cover part of a larger gift.

Annual £3,000 exemption: Lifetime gifts are exempt up to a total of £3,000 in any tax year, this limit being in addition to any number of gifts falling within the normal expenditure and the £250 exemptions. Both husband and wife qualify for this annual exemption. Where gifts fall short of the £3,000 limit the shortfall is carried forward to the following year and added to the allowance for that year only. Unused relief which has been carried forward from the previous year can only be utilised once the current year's annual exemption has been used.

Example

A made capital transfers in 1986/87 of £3,000. In 1987/88 he gave £5,000. Mrs A made transfers of £1,000 in 1985/86, £2,000 in 1986/87 and £5,000 in 1987/88.

The position is as follows:

	A	Mrs A
1985/86	N/A	Exempt
1986/87	Exempt	Exempt
1987/88	£2,000 chargeable	£1,000 chargeable

Mrs A can utilise the balance of her 1986/87 allowance against her 1987/88 transfers, but she cannot carry forward the unused amount from 1985/86.

Exemption for marriage gifts: There is an exemption for gifts in consideration of a marriage. The amount of the exemption depends upon the relationship of the donor to the people being married. The exemptions are as follows:

£5,000   For a parent of either party of the marriage
£2,500   By one party of the marriage to the other or by grandparents or great grandparents.
£1,000   In any other case.

The gift needs to be made *in consideration* of the marriage ie prior to and conditional upon the marriage or on the occasion of the marriage. Strictly speaking the exemption is not available for gifts which are made after the marriage has already taken place.

Gifts into trust

Lifetime gifts to trusts other than those mentioned on p 192 are chargeable at the time of the gift whether or not the donor survives seven years. Inheritance tax is payable at 50 per cent of the normal rates but further tax could be payable if he dies within the following seven years.

What can be done to mitigate IHT?

There are really four simple ideas which you should consider:

- Making use of the £3,000 annual exemption and the exemption for normal expenditure out of income.
- Taking advantage of the seven year rule.
- Drawing up your Will so as to minimise IHT.
- Equalising your estates.

We look at these in turn but they are not mutually exclusive alternatives, there is no reason why you should not use a combination of these. Clearly you would be unwise to jeopardise your financial independence but quite a lot can be achieved by making quite modest provision.

Making use of the £3,000 exemption

Funding the ultimate liability: Substantial sums may be transferred by making full use of this IHT exemption. One possibility is to fund the IHT liability, ie make use of the exemption to fund a life policy which will cover a large part of the eventual IHT liability.

Example

A and his wife are aged 60 and 55 respectively. There is a potential liability for IHT of £100,000 which will arise on the second death. A decided to cover this liability by effecting an insurance policy for the benefit of his children.

An annual premium of approximately £1,270 will be required. In an emergency the plan could be cashed in and it would probably have a surrender value of £11,000 after ten years—possibly more if A or his wife had died.

Note that the payment of £1,270 each year would normally be exempt under the £3,000 annual exemption (or the 'normal expenditure' exemption) and that the policy proceeds of £100,000 would be completely tax free.

If A died after ten years and Mrs A did not wish to continue paying premiums, the £100,000 cover could remain in force for another 14 years—although the policy's surrender value would gradually diminish if this option were taken.

These policies obviously become more expensive the longer you leave them, but not necessarily prohibitively expensive. The premium for a man aged 65 and wife aged 61 would normally be around £1,850 per annum and if you are 70 and 65 when you start, the premiums would still only be of the order of £2,700 per annum.

However, the premiums may have to be 'weighted' if you are in poor health when you take out the policy.

CGT savings

Another possibility is to link up with an important CGT relief. It is possible for a person to give shares or securities on which there is a substantial unrealised capital gain and for a joint election to be made so that the capital gain is 'held over'. In other words, for CGT purposes these shares are deemed to be transferred at their original cost. If the recipient will not otherwise be making use of his annual £6,600 CGT exemption, it may be possible for him to realise the capital gain without CGT being payable.

Example

A (who has already used his CGT annual exemption) has shares which are worth £3,000 but which cost only £500. If he were to sell them he would have a capital gain of £2,500 (ignoring indexation), and tax would be payable of around £750. If A were instead to give the shares to his son, he could 'hold over' the capital gain so that the son would be deemed to have acquired them for £500. A would not then be liable for CGT and the son could escape CGT by realising the investment in a year in which he had not used the annual £6,600 CGT exemption.

Deeds of covenant

Quite often, people feel happier about giving away surplus income rather than making irrevocable transfers of capital. In some cases the pleasure of giving can be increased by the knowledge that the Inland Revenue are having to chip in as well! Payments under deed of covenant are normally exempt for IHT purposes under the exemption for normal expenditure and if the covenant is in favour of a grandchild the recipient may well be able to claim a tax repayment from the Inland Revenue at no additional cost to you.

Basically, everyone, be they six months or 60 years old is entitled to a single person's allowance. Very often minor children will have no income so their allowance goes to waste. Their parents can't remedy this because any income that they transfer to their own children is normally taxed as their income — so they would be no further forward. However, if you transfer income to your grandchildren the income qualifies as their income.

One way of transferring income is by making a deed of covenant — which sounds complicated but isn't. A deed of covenant is merely a legally binding promise in writing that you will pay a specified amount for the next seven years.

Example

A decides to make payments of £1,000 under a deed of covenant to his four grandchildren. They have no other income in their own right.

Instead of paying £1,000 to the children, A actually pays over £730 (ie deducts tax at the basic rate of 27%). The £270 can be recovered from the Inland Revenue so A's gift is increased in value by over 37%. This subsidy can amount to a great deal over seven years!

A does not have to pay the £270 to the Inland Revenue as this is treated as being part of the tax that he pays on his income in the usual way. You should take advice before making large covenants but normally a covenantor's tax position is neutral: your tax bill will be neither increased nor decreased by virtue of your having made a Deed of Covenant.

Taking advantage of the seven year rule

If tax saving is the main consideration, and a person is sufficiently wealthy, it clearly makes sense to give away the nil rate band every seven years. Expressed in another way, all other things being equal, it makes sense for older people to make a transfer of capital as soon as they feel comfortable in doing so, in order to start the seven year period running. Provided that they survive seven years, the gift will be exempt and the individual will have back his nil rate band intact.

The problem which applies for most of us is that we cannot afford to give away as much as the nil rate band. Furthermore, there is the future to be borne in mind, it may be that our widow/widower will need more capital than we can foresee, inflation may go up again and so on. Also we may not be sure which members of our families we wish to have our capital, we may be concerned that having too much capital at a relatively early age will spoil their character, tempt them into extravagance or the wrong sort of company and so on. Therefore, however it might make sense *in theory*, from a tax planning point of view, to give away the nil rate band every seven years, there will very often be good reasons for not wishing to make outright gifts.

A possible solution is to make a discretionary settlement or trust where no one beneficiary has an entitlement to income, but the trustees have discretionary powers to pay income (or capital) to anyone of a class of beneficiaries. In practice, the class of beneficiaries can be quite small and could be limited to your immediate family. This is effectively a way of saving IHT whilst retaining flexibility and control. We have previously mentioned the anti-avoidance rule where the donor reserves a benefit.

The one chink in this seemingly impenetrable obstacle is that it is only the *donor* who must be totally excluded, his wife or widow may be able to benefit. One way of taking advantage of this is to put property into a discretionary trust where the trustees can pay sums to any one of a range of beneficiaries including your spouse. Or it may be appropriate for your spouse to set up a trust which includes you as a beneficiary. But be careful and take advice, there are further anti-avoidance provisions which need to be negotiated if you wish to make use of this possibility. Including your spouse is very much something you should regard as a final fall-back provision in case your circumstances should alter radically.

In any event, forming a discretionary trust of this nature is certainly not a panacea since IHT will be payable on the creation of the trust if it takes you over the £90,000 threshold.

Insurance

It is often possible to effect seven year insurance on very reasonable terms to ensure that your family will be in funds to pay any extra IHT which may be payable if you fail to survive the seven year period.

Example

B has a portfolio worth £150,000. If he puts shares worth £30,000 into trusts he may save IHT of up to £18,000 (depending on the total size of his estate) provided that he survives seven years. Furthermore, IHT will not be charged on any capital growth in the shares he has given away so that if these shares were worth £60,000 after five years, a further saving of IHT will have been achieved. The capital growth will accrue outside B's estate and will escape IHT on B's death even if B does not survive the seven year period.

Costs

A firm of solicitors will need to be involved to draw up the trust deed. In practice their fees should normally be within the range of £250–£600. Capital gains tax need not be payable on the transfer of securities to the trustees provided that the trustees are resident in the UK (the hold-over provisions described on p 197 apply to gifts to trustees as well as to gifts to individuals).

Drawing up your Will to minimise IHT

We have already mentioned the practical advantage of leaving part of the estate in a discretionary trust (see p 186). This was basically recommended in order to use the provision which allows trustees to make appointments within two years of the death and have those payments treated as if they had been contained in the Will. There can, however, also be an advantage in property remaining within a discretionary trust after the two year period has elapsed. A discretionary Will trust can be a way of enabling income and capital to be made available to your widow whilst making use of your nil rate band on your death.

Example

A dies leaving a 65 year old widow and an estate of £330,000. If he leaves his entire estate to Mrs A and she dies five years later the IHT position will be:

IHT on A's death	nil	(covered by spouse exemption)
IHT on Mrs A's death	£99,150	(ie IHT on £330,000).

If A had left Mrs A £240,000 and had left £90,000 in a discretionary Will trust then her income might have been virtually no different. She would have received the income on the £240,000 left to her outright and the trustees of the Will trust might well have appointed most of their income to her. However, from an IHT point of view there would be a considerable improvement. The property held in the discretionary Will trust would not form part of Mrs A's estate on her death so the IHT position would be:

IHT on Mr A's death	nil	(covered by nil rate band)
IHT on Mrs A's death	£57,000	(IHT on £240,000)
	£57,000	

Once again, do bear in mind that you can appoint your widow as a trustee through your Will and this will give her a greater sense of security in that she can count on having the income from the discretionary Will trust.

Equalising your estates

Provided it does not conflict with personal considerations, it makes sense to arrange matters so that your own and your wife's estates are roughly the same value (ie 'equalised'). The point is that your Wills can then be drawn up so as to minimise IHT if some catastrophe should strike you both down in rapid succession. Another point to bear in mind is that you do not know who is going to die first.

The need for this can be shown by the following example:

Example

B and Mrs B have a joint estate of £360,000. However, it is divided unevenly with B owning property worth £330,000 and Mrs B £30,000. If Mrs B dies first and B dies shortly afterwards IHT of up to £102,000 will be payable.

If their estates had been equalised and Mr & Mrs B's Wills had contained 'survivorship' clauses so that property passed to the survivor only if he/she survived six months, the total IHT would have been only £62,000.

19 Off to the sun — retirement abroad

Many people dream of retiring abroad. In this chapter we deal with the following questions:

- What do you have to do to satisfy the Inland Revenue that you are not resident?
- How does the concept of domicile differ from residence and why is this important for Inheritance Tax (IHT) purposes?
- What tax planning steps can be taken in the year in which you leave the UK?
- How will your UK income be taxed when you are non-resident?
- What do you need to find out about the country in which you are going to live?

These are complex matters and you should take professional advice. This chapter only scratches the surface and helps you ask the right questions.

What do you have to do to satisfy the Inland Revenue that you are not resident?

We must begin by examining the rules which govern residence status as it does not necessarily follow that you will cease to be resident in the UK for tax purposes even though you acquire a home abroad. This is crucially important. If an individual continues to be regarded as UK resident he will generally remain subject to UK tax on his worldwide income. On the other hand, if he is not resident for tax purposes his liability will be confined to UK source income such as rents, pensions paid by a former UK employer, dividends from UK companies, interest from both UK companies and UK deposits. Furthermore, a non-resident who is also not ordinarily resident will not normally be subject to CGT (although see later — CGT and sales of business).

Residence

The Inland Revenue practice has evolved in a piecemeal way and is largely based upon decided cases. There is relatively little legislation which bears directly on the matter and what little is said raises almost as many questions as it answers. For example, the Taxes Acts clearly contemplate that an individual can be resident in the UK even though he is absent from the country for the entire year! However, certain aspects of Revenue practice are clearly defined.

Available accommodation

If you have accommodation available for use in the UK, you are resident here for any year in which you as much as set foot in this country. This is the position even if you do not actually use the accommodation. Moreover, the accommodation may be regarded as available even though you do not own it.

A decided case showed that the availability of a shooting lodge in Scotland was sufficient to make a foreigner resident for years when he came to the UK. The retention of a suite of rooms at a hotel or a club could also render you 'resident' if they were kept in a 'permanent state of readiness' for your use.

There is an exception to this general rule if you are working full time abroad — the exemption does not continue after you have retired.

Does this mean that I will have to sell my property in the UK?

Not necessarily; you could let it for instance so that it would not be available for your use although a tax liability would arise on the rents that you received. Or it may be that you can escape by claiming under a Double Tax Treaty. Several of these treaties contain provisions whereby people resident both in the UK and another country may be treated as resident in only one country. But these are exceptions to the general rule that in order to achieve non-resident status you must not have available accommodation.

Visits to the UK

You will be regarded as resident in any tax year if you spend 183 days or more in this country. The Revenue booklet contains the ominous statement: 'There are no exceptions to this rule', although in practice a dually resident individual may still be able to establish that he should be treated under the provisions of a double tax treaty as if he were not resident. The Revenue normally ignores the days of arrival and departure, but there have been cases where fractions of days have been taken into account, so it would be wise to err on the side of caution.

Even if the 183 days test does not apply, you may still be treated as resident if you make regular visits to the UK which average more than three months per tax year, measured over a four year period.

Example

'A' has been resident abroad for a number of years, but begins to make visits to the UK. The periods spent in the UK each year are as follows:

1984/85	51 days
1985/86	98 days
1986/87	170 days

If he spent 45 days or more in the UK during 1987/88 his visits will have averaged 91 days per annum and he will be regarded as having become resident again from 6 April 1987. If he did not visit the UK at all during 1987/88 he will be able to spend 98 days in the UK during 1988/89, as he will then be just within the limit for the period 1985/86–1988/89.

If he spends 45 days or more in the UK during 1987/88 his visits will have averaged 91 days per annum and he will be regarded as having become resident again from 6 April 1987. If he does not visit the UK at all during 1987/88 he will be able to spend 98 days in the UK during 1988/89, as he will then be just within the limit for the period 1985/86–1988/89.

These rules permit some room for manoeuvre in that a continuous period may span two different tax years. It could be, for example, that 'A' spent a single period of 268 days in the UK from 29 December 1985 until 22 September 1986 and still escaped being treated as resident because 98 days fell in the 1985/86 tax year and 170 in 1986/87.

Husband and wife treated separately

Rather surprisingly, since husband and wife are looked at together for most tax purposes, they are taken separately as far as residence is concerned. It is quite conceivable therefore that 'A' could be non-resident but have a resident wife and she would then be treated as a separate person for tax purposes, and income tax and CGT would be charged only on her income and gains.

Do bear in mind, however, that if she has accommodation in the UK this will be regarded as available for her husband's use and this could cause him to be resident here.

Ordinary residence

The CGT legislation imposes a liability on individuals who are resident or ordinarily resident for a year of assessment. Ordinary residence corresponds to *habitual* residence so that an individual may remain ordinarily resident for an isolated year when he happens not to be resident. However, this should not generally be a problem for a person who is retiring abroad as the Inland Revenue will treat a person as not resident or ordinarily resident if he leaves the UK for a period which includes at least three tax years.

Claims under double tax treaties

It is possible for an individual to be simultaneously treated as resident in several countries. A number of double tax treaties contain provisions whereby a dually resident person may be treated as if he were resident in only one country, and set out rules for determining the position. Typically, the tests will be:

(a)   If the individual has a permanent home in only one country that is where he will be deemed to be resident.
(b)   If the position has not been resolved by (a) then the individual is to be treated as resident where he has the centre of his personal and economic interests.
(c)   If the above tests do not resolve the position, the individual is treated as resident where he has an habitual abode.

(d)   If he has an habitual abode in both countries, he is deemed to be a resident of the country of which he is a national.

It will be obvious that these tests can be rather uncertain and if you can so arrange matters, it may be that you should seek to resolve the position by ensuring that you do not have a home in the UK. The centre of your personal and economic interests may be in the UK if your family reside here and most of your income and assets are in the UK. Nevertheless, the provisions of certain double tax treaties may be a useful safety net if you find that you have inadvertently made yourself resident in the UK for a particular year. Unfortunately, not all countries have double tax treaties with the UK and some treaties do not contain these provisions. Countries with relevant clauses in the double tax treaties include France, Italy, Portugal, Spain, Switzerland and the United States.

Procedure

Strictly speaking, you are either resident or non-resident for a complete year of assessment. However, in practice the Revenue treats individuals as not resident and not ordinarily resident for part of a year of assessment. The Revenue summarises its procedure in Booklet IR 20 as follows:

> If a person claims he has ceased to be resident and ordinarily resident in the UK, and can produce some evidence for this (for example, that he has sold his house here and set up a permanent home abroad) his claim is usually admitted provisionally with effect from the day following his departure. Normally this provisional ruling is confirmed after he has remained abroad for a period which includes a complete tax year and during which any visits to this country have not amounted to an annual average of three months.

> If, however, he cannot produce sufficient evidence, a decision on his claim will be postponed for three years and will then be made by reference to what actually happened in that period. During the three intervening years, his tax liability is computed provisionally on the basis that he remains resident in the UK.

> He therefore continues to receive the various income tax reliefs due to a resident of the UK except for any tax year in which he

does not set foot in the UK. His liability is adjusted, if necessary, when the final decision is made at the end of three years.

How does the concept of domicile differ from residence and why is it so important?

In the longer term, your domicile may be of greater effect than your residence status. As we have seen, IHT is charged on certain lifetime transfers and on death. IHT applies to *all* property worldwide if the transferor is domiciled in the UK (whether or not he is resident here), whereas it applies only to transfers of UK assets if the transferor is domiciled abroad. Similarly, there are income and CGT implications since a foreign domiciled individual who is resident in the UK is not chargeable on overseas income and gains unless they are remitted to this country.

Domicile is a different concept from residence. As we have seen, you can be resident in more than one country but you can only have one domicile. You are domiciled where you regard yourself as 'belonging' or (put another way) the place which is your natural and permanent home. Nationality and residence are relevant factors, but are not conclusive in themselves, and it is quite conceivable that a person may reside in a country for a number of years for personal and/or financial reasons and yet still not be domiciled there. There is a difficult onus of proof which needs to be satisfied before the Revenue and the courts will be satisfied that an original domicile has been abandoned and a new 'domicile of choice' has been acquired.

In practical terms, it will be extremely hard for a person of UK origin who is retiring abroad to establish that he has become domiciled there. If a UK property is retained the Inland Revenue will generally conclude that the individual had not finally resolved to live the rest of his life abroad, and that he remains legally domiciled in the UK. The retention — or otherwise — of property in the UK is, however, far from being the only factor in this very complex and subtle matter.

Similarly, if such an individual eventually returns to the UK the Inland Revenue will argue that he was domiciled in this country for the whole of his life, notwithstanding that he spends a long period abroad.

If mitigation of IHT is a serious consideration, then it will be advisable to attempt to establish a foreign domicile as soon as possible as IHT is levied on an individual's worldwide estate if he dies within three years of having had UK domicile. The Revenue's domicile questionnaire is included below. Steps to be taken which may help to establish foreign domicile, according to the *Allied Dunbar Tax Guide*, are:

(1)   Develop a long period of residence in the new country.
(2)   Purchase or lease a home.
(3)   Marry a native of that country.
(4)   Develop business interests there.
(5)   Make arrangements to be buried there.
(6)   Draw up your Will according to the law of the country.
(7)   Exercise political rights in your new country of domicile.
(8)   Arrange to be naturalised (not vital).
(9)   Have your children educated in the new country.
(10) Close current account in UK and open in new country.
(11) Resign from all clubs and associations in your former country of domicie and join clubs, etc in your new country.
(12) Any religious affiliations that you have with your old domicile should be terminated and new ones established in your new domicile.
(13) Arrange for your family to be with you in your new country.

The above are some of the factors to be considered and the more of these circumstances that can be shown to prevail, the sooner you will be accepted as having changed your domicile.

INLAND REVENUE DOMICILE QUESTIONNAIRE

Name: ....   Reference: ....
The following information is requested in order that the claim to be not domiciled in the United Kingdom may be given consideration.

1   Where and when were you born?   _____
2   In what country was your father domi-
    ciled at the date of your birth? (In the
    case of a country with a Federal system,
    the particular State, Province, etc.
    should be stated.)   _____

(Continued overleaf)

3   What changes, if any, took place in your father' domicile during your minority?   _____

4   If your father is dead, state his full name and the date and place of his death.   _____

5   In what country do you consider that you are domiciled and on what grounds? (In the case of a country with a Federal system, the particular State, Province, etc should be stated.)   _____

6   Whether any accommodation is retained for your use in that territory and, if so, the address, the nature of the accommodation and whether it is kept in a permanent state of readiness for your occupation.   _____

7   What are your business, personal, social or other connections with that territory?   _____

8   If you are married, where do your spouse and any children reside?   _____

9   Is any accommodation retained for your use in the United Kingdom and, if so, the address and nature of the accommodation?   _____

10   What periods have you spent in the United Kingdom during each of the past 10 years?   _____

11   The reason for your residence in the United Kingdom, eg whether in connection with business or employment (in which event, details of the business or employment and the nature of the position held should be stated), or the education of children.   _____

12   What are your intentions for the future; and if not to stay permanently in the United Kingdom, the circumstances in which it is envisaged that residence will cease?   _____

Date: ....   Signature: ....
                                        Address: ....
                                                    ....
                                                    ....

What tax planning steps can be taken in the year of departure?

The most important considerations are usually the timing of retirement, departure abroad and the avoidance of CTT problems on the sale of assets such as a business or shares in a family company.

Golden handshakes

Because of the rules which govern top-slicing relief (see p 124) it will be beneficial in many cases for a person to terminate his employment at the very beginning of a tax year during which he retires abroad. The relief will be maximised if you retire on 6 April and then immediately cease to be resident.

Commutation of pension rights

The decision whether to commute all or part of your pension involves a number of considerations. We have found that expatriates who have a guaranteed income via their company pension are generally able to invest their capital in ways which allow it to grow. At the other extreme, expatriates who have no pension income often end up keeping all their capital on deposit — which is almost certainly the wrong policy in the longer term. The reasons for this difference may be partly emotional but we should not ignore this factor and we would, therefore, counsel against surrendering all pension entitlement for a cash sum unless (perhaps) early retirement has been taken.

The tax implications are only one consideration and depend upon the country in which an individual is going to reside. Many countries have double tax treaties which mean that his pension will be taxed only in that country (eg Spain and Portugal) but in other cases there can be a tax advantage in commuting his pension and thus having less income which is taxable in the UK. The expatriate can often then invest his lump sum in a way whereby it attracts tax neither in the UK nor in the country of residence.

Capital gains tax

Sales of main residence

The crucial thing to bear in mind when considering CGT is that it is generally the date on which contracts are exchanged which fixes the date of disposal — not the completion date. So it will not avoid CGT if you exchange contracts whilst you are still resident even though you may have ceased to be resident before you receive payment.

In many cases, it is simply not practical to defer the exchange of contracts until you have left the UK. It may be possible to give your solicitor a power of attorney to act in your absence — but this may also produce practical problems.

Fortunately it will often not matter anyway — generally no chargeable gain arises on the disposal of a main residence, but it is necessary to outline the exceptions to that general rule in case they apply in your particular situation. The flow chart on p 122 should make the position clear.

Sale of a company or business

No CGT will be payable if you dispose of shares in your private company after you have ceased to be resident or ordinarily resident in the UK.

It is more difficult to avoid CGT on the sale of a business. By the very nature of things, a purchaser will wish there to be continuity of trading and will not just be acquiring assets which are used in a trade. Indeed, there will often be a significant element of goodwill in the price, and this definitely requires continuity. The problem is that a vendor will not be able to avoid CGT by deferring a sale until he has ceased to be UK resident as Section 12 CGTA 1979 makes these types of gains subject to CGT if the non-resident has traded in the UK through a branch or agency.

This is a complex area where it would be sensible to take professional advice. Remember that for CGT purposes a disposal takes place when you enter into a contract. An oral contract can sometimes count for these purposes so don't leave it too late before you take advice.

How will your UK income be taxed when you are resident overseas?

As mentioned, liability for income tax on UK income continues even though the recipient is not resident in the UK. Directors' fees from UK resident companies and UK pensions are generally subject to UK tax. Withholding tax is deducted at source at the rate of 27 per cent from dividends and interest (and there is also a liability to higher rate tax). These can sometimes be avoided if there is a double tax treaty in force.

Directors' fees and pensions

Directors' fees and remuneration from UK companies will normally remain subject to income tax. Certain double tax treaties provide a possible exemption which covers other types of earned income, for example the relevant part of the UK–USA Treaty states:

> *Article 14 (Independent personal services).* Income derived by an individual who is a resident of the United States from the performance of personal services in an independent capacity may be taxed in the *USA*. Such income may also be taxed in the UK if (*and only if*):
>
> (*a*) the individual is present in the United Kingdom for a period or periods exceeding in the aggregate 183 days in the tax year concerned, or
> (*b*) the individual has a fixed base regularly available to him in the United Kingdom for the purpose of performing his activities, but only so much thereof as is attributable to services performed in the United Kingdom.
>
> *Article 15 (Dependent personal services)* Remuneration derived by a resident of the United States in respect of employment exercised in the US shall be taxable only in the USA if:
>
> (*a*) the recipient is present in the United Kingdom for a period not exceeding in the aggregate 183 days in the tax year concerned, and
> (*b*) the remuneration is paid by or on behalf of an employer who is not a resident of the United Kingdom, and
> (*c*) the remuneration is not borne as such by a permanent establishment or a fixed base which the employer has in the United Kingdom.

The UK–USA Treaty is chosen because it has served as a model as other treaties have been re-negotiated.

Pensions are also normally subject to UK tax, but here again double tax treaties may provide exemption. The UK–USA Treaty stipulates that pensions paid to a resident of the USA shall be taxable only in the USA unless the pension is paid by the UK government or local authority when it may be taxed in the UK. However, UK tax is not charged if the pensioner is a US national as well as resident in the USA.

Under normal circumstances, government pensions (eg civil

service, armed forces, teachers etc) are always paid after deduction of withholding tax.

Dividends

A non-resident is not normally entitled to the 'tax credit' (ie, tax deducted at source). But, if your investment income is sufficiently large there may be a liability for higher rate tax.

Example

C receives UK dividends of £21,000. If he were resident in the UK he would be entitled to tax credits of 27/73rds, ie £7,767 (these credits can be re-claimed to the extent that the individual is entitled to allowances). However, a non-resident is not normally entitled to claim personal allowances (but see p 217 on claims under S27 of the ICTA 1970) and C may have a higher rate tax liability computed as follows:

Taxable Income   £21,000
Higher Rate Tax Due: £433

The situation may well be different if the individual can claim under a double tax treaty as many of these provide that the recipient can reclaim part of the tax credit and is not subject to higher rate tax. The relief under the treaties generally operates in the following way:

Example

C would be entitled to claim the tax credits and to reclaim half so that the effective rate of UK withholding tax is 14.5%, ie:

UK dividends	£21,000
Tax credits	7,767.00
	£28,767.00
Withholding tax $14\frac{1}{2}$%	3,883.50
Repayment:	
Tax credits	7,767.00
Less: withholding tax	3,883.50
	£3,883.50

Interest

Untaxed interest is theoretically liable to UK tax but the Inland Revenue does not generally pursue such tax. Extra-Statutory Concession B13 states:

> Where a person not resident in the United Kingdom receives interest (eg bank interest) without deduction of income tax and is not chargeable in the name of an agent under Section 78 of the Taxes Management Act 1970, no action is taken to pursue his liability to income tax except so far as it can be recovered by set-off in a claim to relief (eg for proportionate reliefs and allowances under Section 27 of the Income and Corporation Taxes Act 1970) in respect of taxed income from United Kingdom sources.

An agent for these purposes is a person who can instruct the bank etc on payments and transfers from the account.

UK residents normally receive interest net of tax at the composite rate, but this system does not apply to individuals who are not ordinarily resident and they will be able to receive interest gross by signing a certificate confirming to the bank etc that the beneficial owner of the deposit is not ordinarily resident in the UK.

A number of double tax treaties exempt foreigners from UK tax on interest income or specify that UK tax shall not exceed a specified rate.

Countries with relevant treaties include: Italy, France, Malta, Portugal, Spain, Switzerland and the United States.

Exempt gilts

Interest paid on certain British government securities is exempt from income tax provided that the beneficial owner is neither resident nor ordinarily resident in the UK. The relevant securities are listed below. It should be noted that the exemption applies only if the non-resident holds the stock at the date that the interest is paid and does not apply where the non-resident has sold the stock even though the sale may have been 'ex-div'. The Inland Revenue is understood to apply a strict interpretation to the exemption and have denied repayment in such cases.

Application for repayment and for payment of interest without deduction should be made on Forms A1 and A3 obtainable from:

Inspector of Foreign Dividends
Lynwood Road
Thames Ditton
Surrey
KT7 0DP

Gilts exempt from tax for non-UK residents:

$3\frac{1}{2}\%$	War Loan 1952 or after	$9\frac{1}{2}\%$	Treasury 1999
$5\frac{1}{2}\%$	Treasury 2008–12	10%	Treasury 1993
$5\frac{3}{4}\%$	Funding 1987–91	$10\frac{1}{2}\%$	Treasury (CV) 1992
6%	Funding 1993	11%	Exchequer 1990
$6\frac{1}{2}\%$	Funding 1985–87	$12\frac{1}{2}\%$	Treasury 1993
$6\frac{3}{4}\%$	Treasury 1995–98	$12\frac{3}{4}\%$	Treasury 1992
$7\frac{3}{4}\%$	Treasury 1985–88	$12\frac{3}{4}\%$	Treasury 1995
$7\frac{3}{4}\%$	Treasury 2012–15	13%	Treasury 1990
8%	Treasury 2002–6	$13\frac{1}{4}\%$	Exchequer 1996
$8\frac{1}{4}\%$	Treasury 1987–90	$13\frac{1}{4}\%$	Treasury 1997
$8\frac{3}{4}\%$	Treasury 1997	$13\frac{3}{4}\%$	Treasury 1993
9%	Conversion 2000	$14\frac{1}{2}\%$	Treasury 1994
9%	Treasury 1994	$15\frac{1}{4}\%$	Treasury 1996
9%	Treasury 1992–96	$15\frac{1}{2}\%$	Treasury 1998

Rental income

Anybody who rents UK property is required to deduct basic rate tax (27 per cent) from any rents paid to a non-resident landlord and pay the tax to the Revenue. This obligation exists even if the rent is paid into a UK bank account. Moreover, the obligation to deduct basic rate tax applies to the gross amount of the rent, so that if the landlord incurs expenses he is obliged to make a repayment claim. The only way of avoiding these deductions is for the rent to be collected by a UK agent. Rent paid to an agent is paid gross and the agent then becomes liable for assessment. However, the assessment is on the net amount after deducting allowable expenses, so this provides a valuable cash flow benefit.

The following expenses are normally allowable:

● Agent's fees
● Interest on mortgates and similar loans (the £30,000 limit does not apply)
● An allowance of 10 per cent of the net rents for wear and

tear to furniture (subject to the property being let for six months of the year, and being available for letting all year).

Offshore investment companies

If no relief is due under a double tax treaty, and the investment income is sufficiently large to make the individual subject to higher rate tax, it may make sense to transfer the securities to an offshore investment company. There will then be no UK liability beyond the tax withheld at source. It will generally be sensible to carry out such transfers after you have left the UK as there may otherwise be CGT problems.

Personal allowances

You are generally entitled to personal allowances only if you are resident here, although non-resident British subjects may make a claim for a proportion of the allowances to which they would be entitled if they were resident (a claim under *ICTA 1970*, s 27). The way in which this relief is computed is to calculate the income tax liability which would arise if you were UK resident and the whole of your income were subject to UK tax. The resultant figure is then subjected to the fraction $\frac{UK\ Income}{World\ Income}$ and if the product is less than the tax withheld at source from UK income, the individual is entitled to a repayment.

Example

D has UK income of £15,000 and foreign income of £5,000. He is a bachelor and even if he were resident in the UK he would be entitled only to a personal allowance of: £2,425

Relief under s 27 would be computed as follows:

Total income	£20,000 (including foreign income)
Less: personal allowance	2,425
	17,575

Tax on 17,575 = £4,725

$\frac{UK\ Income}{World\ Income} = \frac{15}{20}$ $\frac{15}{20} \times £4,745 = £3,558.93$

UK tax on £15,000 = £4,050.00
Relief under s 27 =   491.07

Tax Payable   £3,558.93

What do you need to find out about the country in which you are going to live?

The above has set out the UK tax position, but it you are retiring abroad you will need to explore carefully the tax system in the country in which you will reside. It is likely that the basic rules for computing assessable income will be quite different from those which apply in the UK and you will obviously need to take competent local advice.

General strategy — finding out more

Tax legislation changes with bewildering frequency, both in the UK and abroad. Once you have decided to retire abroad you should make enquiries via the Embassy concerned about current rates of tax and allowances. The international firms of accountants (Touche Ross, Deloittes, Price Waterhouse, etc) publish information guides on doing business in most developed countries. However, these guides, usually free of charge, are not up-dated every year so you will still need to check with local accountants and advisers. Beware of the mental trap of assuming that the foreign tax system incorporates the same exemptions as our own. For example, since 1 July 1986 we have an exemption from CGT for gilts but you may well find that if you settle in (say) Florida that a CGT liability could arise under US tax legislation. Remember that the base cost for foreign CGT purposes may remain your original cost and not the market value when you take up residence abroad.

Certain countries such as Canada do compute gains in this way but they are the exception rather than the rule.

Another anomaly worth mentioning also arises in connection with gilts. It is the practice on sales of short gilts (less than five years to redemption) for the seller to receive an adjustment which represents the interest which has accrued on a daily basis. This is not at present subject to income tax in the UK (although possible changes are on the way), but if you are resident in the US for example, it does constitute taxable income.

Other financial considerations

The position on UK retirement pensions needs to be carefully explored. After all you have paid in for these benefits for most of your working life! If you have already reached 65 before you retire abroad, there is no problem. You should notify the DHSS so that suitable arrangements can be made. You will, however, have your pension frozen unless you reside in an EEC country or one of those countries which has a reciprocal arrangement with the UK in which case you will continue to qualify for annual increases. The DHSS issue two helpful booklets, SA29 *'Your Social Security and Pension Rights in the European Community'* and N138 *'Social Security Abroad'*.

Even if you have not yet reached the statutory retirement age you will still generally qualify for a National Insurance Retirement Pension in due course, but the amount may be restricted unless you have a full 'contribution record'. There is generally no obligation to pay contributions if you are resident abroad, but it may pay you to make Class 3 voluntary contributions if you are nearing retirement. These will safeguard your right to a full pension. And, provided you reside in an EEC country, they could be a sensible investment in that the benefits will be 'index linked' and the prospective return is, therefore, very attractive.

Foreign exchange controls

These vary immensely, but the current position in the UK is relaxed compared to other countries. There is unlikely to be any problem at the present time if you reside in another EEC country, but even here the position may change according to the political climate. You may well not foresee any likelihood of wishing to return to the UK or moving to another country, but why not keep the position as flexible as possible? Preserve your options as far as possible. Find out when you will become subject to exchange controls (this does not usually happen until you have been resident in a country for several years) and investigate what action you could take (for example making a settlement) which could lessen your exposure.

Inheritance law

Again bear in mind that foreign legal systems are quite different from our own. For example the inheritance laws in Guernsey require a fixed proportion of a deceased person's estate to pass to his children. This kind of rule applies in many continental countries and needs to be borne in mind. Is it what you want to happen? If not, then you need to take legal advice on ways in which you may be able to circumvent these rules, perhaps by making a separate English Will, or creating a settlement.

You should certainly make a Will for each jurisdiction in which you have assets.

Purchase of a property overseas

Property like an investment has its share of pitfalls. Do remember that the legal situation in any country can change overnight. There are, however, some general rules which apply wherever you are thinking of buying. They may sound obvious, but British people have a tendency to do rash things when in an unfamiliar environment. The combination of sunstroke and the local wine can leave the unwary signing things that they would not dream of signing back home.

First and foremost, do *not* try to dispense with the services of a lawyer. On the contrary, sensible people engage one in Britain (usually their own solicitor) and another in the area chosen for their retirement.

Do use a reputable agent, preferably one affiliated to a professional surveying body, or FOPDAC (Federation of Overseas Property Developers, Agents and Consultants, 55 Sidney Street, Cambridge).

Do not part with any money, however much you are impressed by the developer or the agent, other than through a bank or lawyer. Then at least you will have tangible evidence to support your claim to have purchased the property.

Never buy off a plan, unless a large section of the development is already completed. If you must do so, however, insist on a bank or insurance company guarantee of completion. Check the development's water and electricity sources.

The choice of property is so wide and the pressure of the sales pitch so enticing that you must be firmly prepared before you negotiate. Prepare a checklist and make the agent or vendor complete a copy. You should get a majority of ticks and the negatives will help you to reduce the price if it has been pitched artificially high. Even the price of a new property is subject to negotiation, no matter what the brochure says.

You will want to know the details that will have a direct bearing on the lifestyle you wish to enjoy. Particularly if you are looking at an apartment.

(1) Is the development predominantly English occupied or multi-national?
(2) Can I meet one or two of the occupants?
(3) Is membership of any of the following clubs included: beach, riding, golf, country, tennis, bowls?
(4) If not, are there any centres for these sports close by and are there any special concessions on membership fees?
(5) Is there a heated swimming pool?
(6) Is a garage included?
(7) Is there a club room and bar?
(8) Is there a clinic with an English speaking doctor in the complex?
(9) Is there a telephone included or a telephone point?
(10) Is there a bus service to the nearest town?
(11) Is there a taxi point and what is the fare to the nearest town/airport?
(12) What security arrangements exist? 24 hour patrol? Phone linked to a central point?
(13) Is there a television point?
(14) Does it include a mooring?
(15) Is a safe or any furniture included in the price?
(16) Can somebody build in front of the beautiful view?
(17) Will the developer maintain an office on the site?
(18) What are the charges for the upkeep of communal gardens, swimming pool and outside painting, etc? How often are they revised?
(19) Where is the nearest shopping complex and does it contain a pharmacy?
(20) Is the apartment air-conditioned?
(21) Does it include the following: dishwasher, washing machine, refrigerator, waste disposal unit and bathroom heater?

It will be impossible to get 21 ticks but some developments offer most of these benefits and you should be able to score 14 or above. Your own priorities will determine whether these 14 will be sufficient to warrant a purchase.

Having decided that it's the area you like and that the property is also to your liking, we suggest *most strongly* that you pay careful attention to the following list:

(1)   Engage a lawyer — preferably one who is bi-lingual and who understands the propety laws in the country where you wish to live.
(2)   Don't be tempted by the deals which appear to save you money — usually they don't in the long run.
(3)   Check the credentials of the agent and the developer.
(4)   Make sure that the vendor has full and proper title to the property he is setting out to sell you.
(5)   See the property 'in the flesh' — and try to see it 'warts and all', not merely in bright warm sunshine and mild spring breezes. If you're going to live there, you should see it in the winter time.
(6)   Don't over commit yourself financially.
(7)   Make any transfers of money formally, preferably by notorised document, through your own bank and/or lawyer.
(8)   Make sure you're happy to live — all the year round — in the community and area of which your intending property is part.

Finally, do take care and don't sign *anything* until you have sought professional advice. A number of people have lost money in property deals abroad, particularly in Spain, and more often than not their loss has been at the hands of British people and British companies.

20 Homeward bound

This chapter deals with two classes of people who come to the UK from abroad, and addresses the questions:

● What action should UK expatriates take before returning home?

● How should foreigners arrange their affairs if they retire to the UK?

UK expatriates returning home

Expatriates who return to the UK do not generally qualify for any income tax or CGT concessions. They become liable to UK tax on their worldwide income and gains once they become resident and ordinarily resident in the UK. Tax planning in these situations consists mainly in timing the date of return, and ensuring that certain pitfalls are avoided.

The tax position can be very complicated and you would be well advised to take professional advice from an accountant, solicitor etc. You may also find the *Allied Dunbar Expatriate Guide* of value. However, the following checklist etc may be of assistance in putting you on the right lines.

Checklist for expatriates about to return to the UK

● Should capital gains be realised before you resume residence in the UK and become subject to CGT? Will there be a sale of a UK property and, if so, will it be covered by the main residence exemption? (See flowchart on p 122)

● Should capital gains be realised before the start of the tax year in which you return to the UK (this will normally be advisable if you have been non-resident for less than 36 months).

● Should UK bank deposit accounts be closed before the

date of return to avoid UK tax liability on interest? However, consider possible liability for foreign tax.

- Consider a way of 'bringing forward' income on foreign securities etc, eg by selling stocks cum-div and repurchasing ex-div. Should foreign bank deposit accounts be closed immediately before you return to the UK? Again you should bear in mind the possible tax implications in the foreign country in which you are resident.
- Ensure that pay for any terminal leave period will not attract UK tax — normally it will be covered by the 100 per cent deduction.
- There may be cases where liability for VAT can be avoided by arranging for professional advisers to invoice you while you are non-resident.

Golden handshakes (See p 124)

Finally, it is worth mentioning in this context that a special relief may be available for expatriates who return to the UK and receive a golden handshake after their return.

A termination payment is completely exempt where foreign service represents 75 per cent of the total period of employment or (where the employment lasted more than 20 years) at least 50 per cent of the period was spent in foreign service during the last 20 years. The definition of foreign service is that the employee was either not resident or not ordinarily resident or entitled to the 100 per cent deduction as having met the 365 day test.

Example

A was non-resident in the UK from 1969 to 1979. He then qualified for the 100% deduction from 1979 until 1983, so that he was not subject to UK tax on his salary even though he was resident. In 1987 he returned and received compensation of £80,000. $\frac{14 \text{ years}}{18 \text{ years}} = 77\%$ and so the compensation of £80,000 is exempt.

Where the above conditions are not satisfied the employee is entitled to an extension to the £25,000 exemption available to UK residents generally which is determined by the formula:

$$\frac{\text{Foreign service}}{\text{Total period of employment}}$$

This fraction is applied to the amount of the golden handshake after deduction of the £25,000 exemption.

Example

Suppose A's employment had started in 1973. The fraction

$$\frac{\text{Foreign service (10)}}{\text{Total period of employment (14)}}$$

then becomes 71%, so the compensation is not completely exempt. The taxable amount would be arrived at as follows:

Compensation	£80,000
Less: 'normal exemption'	£25,000
	£55,000
10/14ths thereof	£39,286
Taxable amount	£15,714

Example

If A had other taxable income of £28,000 (after allowances and including his salary from the job) the tax payable on the £15,714 would be computed as follows:

Total taxable income £43,714 tax thereon	£17,886
Deduct tax payable on income of £28,000	9,383
	8,503

Tax actually payable on the £80,000 compensation is 50% of £8,503, ie £4,251.50.

Retiring to the UK — a tax haven!

It is a little known fact that the UK is a tax haven for persons of foreign domicile who settle here. If you are not domiciled in the UK and have overseas income and capital gains, you need not pay tax unless you remit them here, so payment of UK tax on overseas income and gains becomes a *voluntary* activity, provided that you can arrange your affairs in the right way!

We have already discussed the concept of domicile (see p 208) and it will be apparent that you may reside in the UK for a number of years and still not be domiciled here. A special rule applies for IHT purposes whereby you will be deemed to be domiciled in the UK if you have been resident for 17 of the preceding 20 tax years, but this rule does not affect the favourable treatment for income tax and CGT purposes.

The most important steps to take from a practical point of view are the establishment of several different offshore bank accounts so that capital and accumulated income can be clearly identified. The point is that if you make remittances to the UK from a 'mixed' account which contains both capital and accumulated income, the Inland Revenue will argue that the remittances are to be identified primarily with income: ie the worst possible basis! However, this potential problem is easily overcome by opening separate offshore bank accounts.

Basically, the balance on your account at the date you come to the UK to take up residence is regarded as capital. In future, overseas income should be credited to a separate account, and this includes interest on your existing overseas bank account. Furthermore, a third account needs to be opened to receive the proceeds of sales of overseas securities and other foreign assets which show capital gains. Other sale proceeds should be credited to your main capital account.

Obviously, your strategy should be to live off your capital account, and to supplement this (if necessary) by remittances from the account which contains capital gains. Only as a last resort should you make remittances from the income account if they take your taxable income over the personal allowance. In this way you will legitimately have minimal overseas income and gains to declare.

Furthermore, there are a number of ways in which you can use the balance on your overseas income account without incurring a UK tax liability. Firstly, you can spend the money outside the UK (for example on holidays) or you can invest it (but be careful of the way in which you deal with the position when you sell the investment or you may end up remitting income without meaning to do so). In an emergency you should be able to rely on court decisions which indicate that a husband who gives his wife accumulated overseas income is not liable to income tax when she remits it, as it is capital in her hands! However, you should take professional advice before doing this in view of the recent trend of House of Lords' decisions (the *Furniss* case again).

Another point which is worth bearing in mind, but needs careful handling, is that if you have just one overseas investment and you sell it, it is arguable that accumulated income from this particular source may be safely remitted in the following tax year. It would be sensible to discuss this with your accountant or professional adviser first, but this is another possible way of remitting money to the UK without incurring an income tax liability.

A foreign domiciled person is still liable to tax in the normal way on income and gains arising in the UK, so you should avoid UK investments. If you wish to invest in the UK Stock Market the best way is to do so via an offshore fund in the Isle of Man or Channel Islands and many unit trust and investment groups have funds which meet this requirement.

An individual can realise chargeable capital gains up to a certain level each year without any CGT liability because they are covered by the annual exemption. Therefore, if you have no UK capital gains it may be wise to remit an appropriate part of the capital gains account. This will then avoid a tax liability if you should need to draw heavily on this account in a later year.

Inheritance tax planning

Until the 17 year rule bites (see p 189) you will not be subject to IHT on capital transfers of foreign assets. Foreign assets include money held in overseas bank accounts, shares in foreign companies and bearer securities actually held overseas. It may well be wise to hold UK property through a foreign investment company as the shares in such a company are 'excluded property' (ie, not subject to IHT when owned by a person of foreign domicile), and this effectively converts UK assets into foreign property. As the 17 year deadline approaches, it may also be appropriate to make a settlement of overseas assets as this will take them outside the ambit of IHT even though you may subsequently be deemed to have UK domicile. Substantial savings of IHT are possible by taking steps of this nature, but it is essential to take competent professional advice.

Glossary

AVC

Additional voluntary contributions to an employer's pension scheme (See p 93). These contributions are paid from your income into your company pension scheme. There will also be separate AVC schemes available from insurance companies and other financial institutions from October 1987.

Accumulation and maintenance trusts

See p 192. A special type of trust which is favourably treated for IHT purposes.

Age relief

See p 118. A tax allowance available to those aged 65 or more provided that their income does not exceed certain limits.

Annuities

See p 154. A policy sold by an insurance company under which you (and possibly your wife) receive a stated sum for the rest of your life.

Buy-out bonds

See p 97. An arrangement under which an individual can take his entitlement under a former employer's pension scheme.

Commuting pension

See p 109. A pension is commuted when the individual takes tax-free lump sum in lieu of all or part of his entitlement.

Deed of covenant

See p 198. A written agreement under which a person promises to pay a specified amount for a period of years. The usual periods are four years for charitable deeds and seven years for deeds of covenant payable to another person.

Deed of family arrangement

See p 187. An agreement reached by beneficiaries of a person's estate under which the provisions of his Will are varied for tax and personal financial planning reasons.

Discretionary trust

This is a type of trust where the trustees do not have to pay income to a particular beneficiary but can choose each year how they allocate income to members of a class of potential beneficiaries.

Domicile

See p 208. Domicile is not necessarily connected with where you presently live, and should not be confused with residence. Domicile is, broadly, the territory which can be regarded as your natural home and in which (apart from occasional absences) you intend to remain indefinitely. Your domicile of origin is determined at birth and, in most circumstances, you will be the domicile of your father. Domicile is not necessarily determined by nationality or by place of birth, though these will in many cases be the same as your domicile. Most UK expatriates are, therefore, of UK domicile.

Double taxation agreements

See p 206. These provide relief to an individual who has income which arises in a foreign country especially where the income is being taxed in that country. Relief can be given either by offsetting the foreign tax paid when calculating taxable income, or by averaging the overall tax payable at the rate applicable here. Similar arrangements may cover people who retire overseas and have income arising in the UK (Note that not all countries have a treaty with the UK).

Earnings rule

See p 129. The rule which governs how much a person can earn after retirement without his state pension being affected.

Equities

See p 158. This is a general name given to ordinary shares issued by quoted companies. Their value rises and falls according to the company's trading results, the Stock Market in general etc. The term equity is meant to distinguish such investments from loan stocks and other fixed interest investments.

Estate

See p 189. This is a technical term for the property which you own at the date of death and trust property where you are entitled to any income.

Executors

See p 185. People who administer a Will.

Exempt gilts

See p 215. These are gilts (qv) where the interest is exempt from UK tax if the owner is not resident or ordinarily resident in the UK.

Frozen pension

See p 96. Pension benefits arising from a former employment which will become payable when the individual reaches retirement age.

Gilts

See p 146. Also known as UK government stocks. These are loan stocks issued by HM Government. They usually carry a fixed rate of interest and are redeemable at a particular date. Some gilts are, however, linked to inflation, ie 'index-linked' gilts.

Golden handshake

See p 124. A lump sum paid voluntarily on an employment ceasing. Also known as termination payments.

Gross fund

One that is not subject to tax, for example a pension scheme.

Inheritance tax (IHT)

See p 189. Death duty, replaced capital transfer tax (which replaced estate duty) in March 1986.

Insurance bonds

Sec p 163. An investment which takes the form of a non-qualifying insurance policy. These investments work in a similar way to unit trusts, although the tax treatment is quite different.

Intestacy

See p 183. This applies where a person dies without making a valid Will.

Managed funds

See p 166. A term commonly used to describe unit linked funds offered by insurance companies. Money invested in bonds and maximum savings plans may be put into such a fund, where the insurance company seeks to achieve a balanced portfolio with some of the fund being invested in property, equities, foreign companies, gilts and cash deposits.

Maximum investment plan

See p 99. A qualifying ten year endowment insurance policy.

Net relevant earnings

See p 95. Earnings from a non-pensionable employment or business less certain deductions such as expenses, trading losses, capital allowances etc.

National Savings Certificates

See p 151. These are investments offered by the Government which provide a tax free return over periods of up to five years.

Personal pension plan

See p 111. Also known as Retirement Annuity Contributions, or as an SEPC policy (Self Employed Pension Contributions).

Residence

See p 204. A concept used to determine under which country's taxation laws you are liable. Although there are complex and differing rules, residence is generally determined by where you actually live in any tax year. In circumstances where this is not clear, you are likely to be declared resident for tax purposes in any country in which you spend more than six months in any tax year (although the legislation differs from country to country, 183 days is the period often adopted for determining residence).

Reservation of benefit

See p 194. If a person gives property away but reserves benefit the gift is null and void for IHT purposes.

Offshore 'roll-up' funds

See p 102. Mutual funds (similar in concept to unit trusts) based in a tax haven such as the Isle of Man or the Channel Islands. Income earned on the fund's portfolio is not paid out as dividends but is accumulated or 'rolled-up'.

Open market options

See p 112. These are options under personal pension plans whereby the individual can 'shop around' at the time of his retirement and transfer the value of his contributions to the company which offers the best annuity rates.

Salary sacrifice

See p 94. An arrangement whereby an individual gives up some of his salary, with the amount that has been given up being paid into a pension scheme.

SERPS

See p 106. State earnings related pension scheme.

Transfer values

See p 97. A payment made from a former employer's pension scheme to secure benefits under your present employer's pension scheme.

Unit trusts

See p 160. A type of investment where investors join together to invest via a 'fund'.

Appendix

Leaflets available from any HM Inspector of Taxes Office

Subject	Reference number
Income Tax and Pensioners	IR 4
Income Tax—Age Allowance	IR 4A
Residents and Non-residents—Liability to tax in the United Kingdom	IR 20
Income Tax Tables	IR 21
Income Tax—Personal Allowances	IR 22
Income Tax and Widows	IR 23
Starting in Business	IR 28
Income Tax and Married Couples	IR 31
Income Tax—Separate Assessment	IR 32
Employed or Self-employed?	IR 56
Thinking of Working for Yourself	IR 57
Capital Gains Tax—Owner-Occupied houses	CGT 4
Capital Gains Tax (a comprehensive booklet)	CGT 8
Capital Gains Tax and the Small Businessman	CGT 11
Capital Gains Tax—Indexation: Financial Act 1982	CGT 12

Index

Abbeyfield Society 9, 15–16
Abroad. *See* Retirement abroad
Accommodation. *See* Housing
Action Resource Centre 23
Activities
   amusing yourself 16–17
   attitudes and 10–17
   gainful 13–15
   voluntary 13–14, 15–16
Addresses 23, 181–182
Age Concern 23, 181
Alcohol tolerance 45
Amusing yourself 16–17
Annuities
   home income schemes 155–156
   investment in 154–155
Anxieties 19–22
Arthritis 39–40
Association of Researchers into Voluntary Action and Community Involvement
   (ARVAC) 23
Attitudes and activities 10–17

BUPA Hospitals 18
BUPA Medical Centres 66
Bereavement 17, 26, 34
Bowel trouble 44
Breast cancer 65–66
Building societies 145–146
Bungalows 74–75
Business
   sale of 121, 126–127
   starting new 131–134

Cancer
   breast 65–66
   prostate 67
Capital
   for home improvements 181
   tax efficient investments 101–103

Capital gains tax
  allowable deductions 121, 123
  annual exemption 123
  chargeable assets 120–121
  indexation allowance 121, 123
  liability 119–120
  main residence exemption 120, 121, 122
  rate 119
  retirement abroad 211–212
  sale of company or business 121, 126–127
Cash
  commuting company pension for 109–110
Cataract 48
Chattels
  exempt from CGT 120
Choice 7, 14, 48
Citizens Advice Bureaux 16, 181
Company
  pension scheme 92–94, 108–113
  sale of 121, 126–127
Coronary heart disease 43–44, 66
Council of Voluntary Services 16

DHSS leaflets 182
Day centres 15
Death
  charge to IHT on 189–191
Debts
  exemption from CGT 120
Deed of covenant 198–199
Deed of variation 187–188
Demographic scene 6–10
Dentistry 57–62
Diet
  digestion and 43–45
  salt 45–46
Digestion 43–45
Directors' fees and pensions 213–214
Disability
  rehabilitation from 39–40
Distressed Gentlefolk's Aid Association 181, 182
Dividends 214
Domicile 208–210
Double tax treaties 206–208
Dwelling house
  main residence exemption 120, 121, 122
  See also Housing

Earnings
  effect on state pension 129–130
  part-time 131
  rule 8

Employer
  former, pension received from 96–98
Employment Fellowship 23
Equity investments 157–167
Executors 185–186
Expatriates returning home 223–225

Falls 40
Family Planning Association 36
Family relationships 5, 19–21
Finance
  advance planning 89–91
  drawing up budget 85–86
  funding retirement 89–104
  managing money 135–143
  pension scheme. *See* Pension scheme
  person about to retire 87
  person concerned to pass on money 87–88
  person planning ahead 86–87
  personal equity plan 100
  planning 83–85
  saving out of surplus income 99–103
Fitness For Industry 37
Flats 74–75
Fluid intake 44–45
Foreign
  currency 121
  exchange controls 219
  inheritance law 219–220
Funding retirement 89–104

Gainful activity 13–15
Gilts
  exempt 215–216
  exemption from CGT 120
  index-linked 149–150
  interest rates 146–149
  investment strategy 176–177
Glaucoma 48
Glossary 229–233
Golden handshakes 211, 224–225
Government stock. *See* Gilts
Grandparent
  exploited 13
  role as 5, 20, 33
Granny flat 9, 10
Grieving 34
Gynaecological problems 64–65

HM Inspector of Taxes leaflets 234
Health
  arthritis 39–40

Health (*continued*)
  breast cancer 65–66
  diet 43–46
  digestion 43–45
  female problems 64–66
  gynaecological problems 64–65
  hearing. *See* Hearing
  keeping in good trim 41
  male problems 66–67
  mental outlook 25–28
  mobility 39–41
  physical fitness 37–46
  relaxation 29–30
  rheumatism 39
  salt consumption 45–46
  sex after sixty 34–36
  sight 47–48
  sleep 30–31
  stress 28–30
  symptoms 41–43
  teeth 57–62
  warning signs 41–43
Hearing
  action to be taken 50–51
  aids 51–52
  deterioration in 48
  onset of loss 49–50
  other aids to 52–53
  tinnitus. *See* Tinnitus
Help the Aged 181
Hospital treatment 180
Housework 21–22
Housing
  bungalows 74–75
  capital idea 181
  finding new home 72–74
  flats 74–75
  general note 69–70
  granny flat 9, 10
  improvements 181
  life on level 74–75
  mobile homes 75–76
  moving 9–10, 17–19, 70–72
  not-so-sheltered 76–78
  sheltered 76–78
  sources of further information 78–79
  staying put 70–72
Hysterectomy 64

Income
  low 179–182
  rental 216–217

Income (*continued*)
  saving out of surplus 99–103
Income tax
  age allowance 118
  computation 115–119
  investment bonds 118–119
  part-time earnings 131
  retirement abroad. *See* Retirement abroad
Inflation
  evaluation of investments 141–143
  pensions and 110–111
Inheritance tax
  agricultural property relief 192
  business property relief 191–192
  charge on death 189–191
  deeds of covenant 198–199
  drawing up will to minimise 201–202
  gifts
    for national purposes 191
    into trust 196–198
    to charities 191
  main exemptions 191–201
  planning 227
  seven year rule 199–201
  transfers to spouse 191
  treatment of lifetime gifts 192–196
Injury
  rehabilitation from 39–40
Insurance company schemes 153–156
Insurance policies
  exemption from CGT 121
Interest
  bearing investments. *See* Investments
  retirement abroad 215
Intestacy 183–184
Invalidity benefit 112–113
Investment bonds
  flexibility 167
  managed funds 166–167
  minimum initial investment 163
  partial cashing in 164–165
  property funds 165–166
  structure 163–164
  tax on cashing in 164
  top slicing relief 118–119
  types of fund 165–167
Investment strategy
  considerations 169–171
  consistency counts 173–174
  general principles 171–178
  management 172
  taxation 174–175

Investment strategy (*continued*)
  unit trusts 172–173
Investments
  analysis 139–140
  bonds. *See* Investment bonds
  capital 101–103
  effect of personal circumstances 137–139
  equity 157–167
  interest bearing
    annuities 154–155
    annuity home income schemes 155–156
    building societies 145–146
    government stock 146–150
    index-linked government stock 149–150
    insurance company schemes 153–156
    meaning 145
    National Savings. *See* National Savings
    off-shore roll-up funds 150
  main criteria for evaluating 135–143
  property 157–167
  strategy. *See* Investment strategy
  unit trusts 160–163
  your own portfolio 160

Leaflets 182, 234
Local authorities 180–181
London Voluntary Service Council 23
Loneliness 4

Managing money 135–143
Marriage Guidance Council 36
Max Planck Institute 25
Meals on Wheels 15
Memory 26–27
Men
  special problems 66–67
Menopause 64–65
Mental outlook
  framework 25–28
  relaxation 29–30
  stress 28–30
Mobile homes 75–76
Mobility 39–41
Motor cars
  exemption from CGT 121
Moving house 9–10, 17–19, 70–72

National Corporation for Care of Old People 6
National Council for Single Women and her Dependants 23
National Council for Voluntary Organisations 23
National Insurance contributions 132

National Savings
  certificates 121, 151–152, 177
  deposit bond 151
  income bonds 151
  index-linked certificates 152
  indexed income bond 151
National Trust 15
Non-person
  danger of becoming 4

Obesity 43
Occupational pension scheme 92–94, 108–113
Offshore investment companies 217
Offshore roll-up funds 150
Open market options 112
Ordinary residence 206–208
Organisations 23, 181
Osteo-arthritis 40

Part-time work 8
Passing on wealth 189–202
Pension
  and inflation 110–111
  choice of 108–109
  commuting
    for cash 109–110
    whether worthwhile 110–113
  directors' 213–214
  effect of deferring 130–131
  last minute arrangements 103–104
  last minute contributions 127
  planning 105–113
  portable 97
  received from former employer
    buy-out bonds 97
    future legislation 97–98
    improvement on 96–98
    transfer values 97
  scheme. *See* Pension scheme
  state. *See* State pension
  supplementary 179–180
  widow's 112
  wife's 98–99
Pension scheme
  advantages 91
  as tax efficient form of saving 91–92
  company 92–94, 108–113
  occupational 92–94, 108–113
  open market options 112
  personal 94–95, 111
  private 92–94, 108–113
  salary sacrifice 94

Pension scheme (*continued*)
  self-employed 96
  types available 92–96
Personal equity plan 100
Personal pension scheme 94–95, 111
Physical fitness 37–46
Pre-Retirement Advisory Committee 6
Pre-Retirement Association (PRA) 3, 6, 11, 17, 21
Private pension scheme 92–94, 108–113
Professional people
  employment of 13
Property
  purchase overseas 220–222
Prostate trouble 66–67

Reaction time 27–28
Relationships
  importance of 31–34
  review of 5
  strain imposed by retirement 19
  with family 5, 19–21
  with spouse 5, 19
Relaxation 29–30
Rental income 216–217
Residence
  available accommodation 204
  domicile distinguished from 208–210
  husband and wife treated separately 206
  ordinary 206–208
  satisfying requirements of non-resident 203–204
  visits to UK 205–206
Retirement
  abroad. *See* Retirement abroad
  accommodation in. *See* Housing
  choosing right date 124
  facing 3–6
  financial aspects. *See* Finance
  funding 89–104
  on low income 179–182
  planning 11–12
  pre-retirement checklist 5
  problems and priorities 3–23
  timing of 125–126
  to UK 225–227
  year of
    checklist for 128
    minimising tax in 127
Retirement abroad
  disadvantages 6
  domicile distinguished from residence 208–210
  finding out about country 218–222
  foreign exchange controls 219

Retirement abroad (*continued*)
   income tax after 212
      directors' fees and pensions 213–214
      dividends 214
      exempt gilts 215–216
      interest 215
      liability 212
      offshore investment companies 217
      personal allowances 217
      rental income 216–217
   inheritance law 219–220
   ordinary residence 206–208
   purchase of overseas property 220–222
   residence 203–206
   tax planning in year of departure 210–212
Rheumatism 39
Roles 19–22
Royal United Kingdom Beneficient Association 181, 182

Salary sacrifice arrangement 94
Salt consumption 45–46
Self-employment
   pension 96
   state pension 108
   tax advantages 9
Sex after sixty 34–36
Sheltered housing 76–78
Sight 47–48
Sleep 30–31
Spouses
   equalising estates 202
   life expectation 9
   relationships with 5, 19
   residence 206
   sex after sixty 34–36
   transfers to 191
State pension
   basic retirement pension 106
   earning without affecting 129–130
   effect of deferring 130
   graduated pension 106
   self-employed persons 108
   state earnings related scheme 106–108
   what can be expected 105
Stress 28–30
Strokes
   rehabilitation from 39–40
Supplementary pension 179–180
Surplus income
   saving out of 99–103
Symptoms 41–43

Tax planning
    checklist for year of retirement 128
    choosing right retirement date 124
    in year of departure abroad 210–212
    inheritance tax 227
    minimising tax 127
    sale of business or company 126–127
    timing of retirement 125–126
    top slicing relief 124–125
Taxation
    capital gains tax 119–123
    cashing in investment bond 164
    double tax treaties 206–208
    importance of 115–128
    income tax 115–119
    investment strategy 174–175
    investments 140–141
    planning. *See* Tax planning
    starting new business 131–134
    working out tax bill 115–123
Teeth 57–62
Tinnitus
    acoustical management 56
    action to be taken 55–57
    meaning 54–55
    pharmacological management 57
    psychological management 56
    symptomatic treatment 55–56
Top slicing relief
    on investment bonds 118–119
    tax planning 124–125

Unit trusts
    investment strategy 172–173
    success of structure 160–161
    tax treatment 162–163
    types of fund 161–162
Universal Beneficient Society 181, 182
Useful addresses 23

Visits to UK 205–206
Voluntary activity 13–14, 15–16

Warning signs 41–43
Widow's pension 112
Wife
    funding pension for 98–99
    working 63–64
    See also Women
Will
    choosing executors 185–186
    discussion of 21

Will (*continued*)
    formalities 184–188
    importance of flexibility 186–187
    intestacy 183–184
    making 183–188
    minimising IHT 201–202
    variation of 187–188
Women
    breast cancer 65–66
    gynaecological problems 64–65
    life expectation 9
    special problems 63–66
    working wife 63–64